Pragmatic Naturalism: John Dewey's Living Legacy

RICHARD J. BERNSTEIN

In memory of John E. Smith
who first introduced me to Dewey's pragmatic naturalism

CONTENTS

ACKNOWLEDGMENTS

I want to thank the editors of the *Graduate Faculty Philosophy Journal* for permission to reprint my essay as a book and for their meticulous editing of my original manuscript. Anantha Krishna Boddapati, the primary editor of my manuscript, checked the accuracy of every reference and made many concrete suggestions to improve my essay. My research assistant Olga Knizhnik helped in innumerable ways from the very inception of writing my essay. She is primarily responsible for transforming my essay into a book. The cover design is a sketch of the young John Dewey based upon an 1893 photograph of Dewey at the Glenmore Summer School of Philosophy, Keene Valley, New York. José Paúl Pérez Cóndor drew the sketch.

PREFACE

This essay was originally published in the centennial issue of the *Graduate Faculty Philosophy Journal* celebrating the founding of The New School for Social Research in 1919. Several colleagues suggested that I publish this essay as a book in order to make it more widely available. John Dewey was one of the founders of The New School, and his spirit has shaped the character of this institution. In the 1950s, when I was a graduate student at Yale University, I wrote my dissertation on Dewey titled "John Dewey's Metaphysics of Experience." This was the time when philosophical interest in Dewey and the pragmatic tradition in general was at an all-time low in the American philosophy departments. Pragmatism had been relegated to the dustbin of history in light of the new developments in analytic philosophy. I felt then that Dewey was actually ahead of his time and that the day would come when philosophers would realize this. In the past few decades, there has been an international resurgence of interest in Dewey and the pragmatic tradition, and today, there is more creative discussion of Dewey and pragmatism than at any time in the past.

John Dewey clearly identified himself as a pragmatic naturalist and was among a number of the early twentieth-century American philosophers who advocated a naturalist orientation in philosophy. This vital philosophical movement had eclipsed, but beginning in the mid-twentieth century, there was a new surge of interest in naturalism stimulated in part by the work of W.V.O. Quine and Wilfrid Sellars. Today, many (perhaps most) American philosophers advocate some version of naturalism, but discussion of what "naturalism" means and what it entails has been almost chaotic. Defenders and critics of naturalism present wildly different conceptions of naturalism.

I argue that despite the plethora of conceptions of naturalism, one can discern—in the revival of liberal naturalisms—a development that is very much in the spirit of Dewey's pragmatic naturalism. This is evident in the work of both the philosophers who have been influenced by the pragmatic tradition and those who do not refer to Dewey or to pragmatism. This recent development vindicates my original intuition that philosophers would eventually catch up with Dewey. What is impressive about this development is the analytic sophistication that contributes to the articulation of Dewey's pragmatic naturalistic vision—particularly in such philosophers as Hilary Putnam, Sellars, Philip Kitcher, Bjorn Ramberg, Peter Godfrey-Smith, Huw Price, David Macarthur, Mark Johnson, Robert Sinclair, Steven Levine, and Joseph Rouse, among many others. After presenting a sketch of Dewey's naturalism, I consider some versions of liberal naturalism in order to show how they contribute to a fine-grained articulation of Dewey's vision of pragmatic naturalism. As I hope to demonstrate, Dewey's legacy is very much alive today.

1 INTRODUCTION

One of the most widely discussed and contentious topics in Anglophone philosophy today is naturalism. At first glance, the discussion and disputes seem chaotic with little agreement about the meaning of "naturalism." There has been a promiscuous proliferation of adjectival characterizations of naturalism: "metaphysical," "ontological," "substantive," "methodological," "reductive," "bald," "liberal," "subject," "object," etc. The list goes on and on, and includes what sounds like an oxymoron—"transcendental naturalism."[1] Anyone who takes up the topic of naturalism today should heed the warning of Barry Stroud:

> The idea of "nature," or "natural" objects or relations, or modes of investigations that are "naturalistic," has been applied more widely, at more different times and places, and for more different purposes than probably any other notion in the whole history of human thought. . . . What is usually at issue is not whether to be "naturalistic" or not, but rather what is and what is not to be included in one's conception of "nature." That is the real question, and that is what leads to deep disagreement.[2]

Stroud also points out that in debates about naturalism there are two opposing pressures:

> [The] pressure on the one hand to include more and more within your conception of "nature," so that it loses its definiteness and restrictiveness. Or, if the conception is kept fixed and restrictive, there is the pressure on the other hand to distort or even to deny the very phenomena that a naturalistic study—and especially a naturalistic study of human beings—is supposed to explain.[3]

Stroud is right about these opposing pressures. But the moral to be drawn is not to abandon the appeal to naturalism, which I suspect is impossible, but rather to be careful in explaining and justifying one's understanding of naturalism.

Taking account of Stroud's warnings and the seemingly endless proliferations of the adjectival descriptions of different types of naturalism, I want to argue that there are powerful tendencies in recent discussions that endorse what is sometimes called "liberal naturalism."[4] This liberal, open, pluralistic naturalism is very close to the spirit (if not always to the letter) of John Dewey's naturalism, especially as developed in *Experience and Nature.*[5] Although some philosophers such as Kitcher, Godfrey-Smith, Price, Macarthur, Sinclair, Ramberg, and Putnam explicitly refer to pragmatism and Dewey in their discussions of naturalism, others, such as Rouse—who does not mention Dewey—nevertheless advance a version of philosophical naturalism that looks like Dewey brought up to date. Putnam draws the connection between liberal naturalism and Dewey's naturalism in one of the last papers that he wrote, "Naturalism, Realism, and Normativity."[6] Putnam notes—with reference to the introduction to *Naturalism in Question* by Mario De Caro and Macarthur—that they

> pointed to and celebrated the existence of a number of philosophical positions that are "naturalist" in the sense that John Dewey, the most famous naturalist philosopher of his period, was—namely, in the sense of rejecting all appeals to supernatural entities in philosophy while simultaneously rejecting the positivist demand that aesthetic and ethical concepts be reduced to the concepts of the natural sciences or expecting that they could, or eventually will be, so reduced. Nor do they accept the positivist view that history will eventually become a "science." . . . De Caro and Macarthur emphasized that the liberal naturalism they advocate doesn't regard normative utterances as somehow "second grade" or merely "expressive," but neither does it countenance a Platonic realm of normative facts independent of human practices and needs. At the same time, it does not countenance Moorean quasi-mystical faculties of moral intuition. All this I like very much.[7]

"Liberal naturalism" does not designate a single position but rather a plurality of stances—and there are still many important controversial issues among liberal naturalists. When Putnam speaks of Dewey as "the most famous naturalist philosopher of his period," he is referring to a philosophical movement that dominated American philosophy during the early decades of the twentieth century—a movement that has been almost totally forgotten and obliterated. Apart from Dewey, this movement included thinkers such as Sidney Hook, Ernest Nagel—both Dewey's students—, George Santayana, Roy Wood Sellars (Wilfrid's father), and Morris Cohen, among many others. When Dewey moved from the University of Chicago to Columbia University in 1904, he was greatly influenced by Frederick Woodbridge, who revived a modern version of Aristotelian naturalism.[8]

Although there were sharp disagreements among these thinkers, they also shared a number of commitments, which they articulated in different ways. Rouse, in his recent book, *Articulating the World*, lists three core commitments of a naturalistic self-understanding.[9] First, naturalists reject "any appeal to or acceptance of what is supernatural or otherwise transcendent to the natural world" (AW 3). The definition of the supernatural and the boundary between the natural and the supernatural is itself contested. The American naturalists were not only critical about the appeal to a transcendent god to explain the world, but they were also critical about the appeal to a "supernatural" faculty of pure reason. Second, naturalists are committed to regarding "scientific understanding as relevant to all significant aspects of human life and only countenance ways of thinking and forms of life that are *consistent* with that understanding" (ibid.). All the American naturalists shared this second commitment, although they differed in their conceptions of what constitutes scientific understanding. Third, "naturalists repudiate any conception of 'first philosophy' as prior to or authoritative over scientific understanding" (ibid.).[10] Philosophy is not to be conceived of as a special discipline that supersedes or competes with the sciences. The American naturalists also shared an additional commitment. They were deeply influenced by Darwin and the style of thinking introduced by evolutionary biology. The philosophical significance of the new biology supported an understanding of human beings as continuous with the rest of nature. Throughout the natural world there

are important distinctions to be drawn, but there are no metaphysical or epistemological dualisms. The naturalism of the American
naturalists was not scientistic or reductionistic; they emphasized
continuity with differences throughout nature.

With the rise and development of analytic philosophy in the
tradition of Frege, Russell, Moore, Carnap, and the Tractarian
Wittgenstein, this early chapter of American naturalism was relegated to the dustbin of history. From the perspective of early
analytic philosophers, the American naturalists lacked any deep or
sophisticated understanding of the new developments in logic initiated by Frege and Russell. "Naturalism" had a *pejorative* meaning
for analytic philosophers, shaped by Frege's conception of pure
logic. Naturalism blurred the distinction between formal logic and
the empirical sciences—especially empirical psychology. All of
this changed in the mid-twentieth century with the work of Quine
and Sellars. Quine not only challenged the foundations of logical
empiricism, he repudiated any claim to "first philosophy" that has
priority over scientific knowledge.[11] He challenged the very idea
of drawing a sharp line between philosophic analysis and empirical science.[12] Quine is famous for his expression "epistemology
naturalized," which indicates that the traditional issues of epistemology should be replaced by empirical scientific inquiry.[13] Sellars
affirms a version of scientific naturalism quite boldly when he declares:

> But, *speaking as a philosopher*, I am quite prepared to say that
> the commonsense world of physical objects in Space and
> Time is unreal—that is, there are no such things. Or, to put
> it less paradoxically, that in the dimension of describing and
> explaining the world, science is the measure of all things,
> of what is that it is, and of what is not that it is not.[14]

Ever since the rise of modern science in the seventeenth century, there have been thinkers who have claimed that science—
especially the natural sciences—are *exclusively* the basis for our
knowledge of the world and the measure of what is truly real.
Whenever this form of scientific naturalism has been pressed to
the extreme, there have always been thinkers who have protested

that such a view is not only mistaken but perverse. The most famous philosopher to make this claim was Kant. Kant acknowledges that human beings are natural creatures and as such they are subject, like the rest of nature, to strict deterministic laws of nature. But, in his critical philosophy, Kant argues that we are not *exclusively* natural creatures. Human beings are also rational beings, capable of both theoretical and practical reason. Kant's Copernican Revolution is intended to show that the very possibility of natural science presupposes the categories, judgments, and regulative ideas of reason. To understand the distinctive character of reason, we need to engage in a critique of reason and elaborate a transcendental philosophy that demonstrates the universality and necessity of pure reason. There is no reason without *normativity*. Consequently, it is impossible—logically impossible—to give an account of reason (both *Verstand* and *Vernunft*) by an appeal to empirical natural science.[15]

We shall see that although the battle lines change, the war between those who claim that the natural sciences are all we need for genuine knowledge of the world and those who argue that the natural sciences alone cannot provide an adequate account of our normative, theoretical, and practical capacities and abilities persists until the present. De Caro and Macarthur give a contemporary formulation of this problem:

> Normativity concerns what we should or ought to do and our evaluations of things or states of affairs. We normally say, for example, that one ought to keep one's promises, that if one accepts *p* and "If p, then q," one ought to accept *q*, or that Mozart was a better musician than Salieri. Plausibly, the sciences describe how things are, particularly the causal powers or causal regularities that exist in the world, lawlike or otherwise. Consequently, if one follows modern Scientific Naturalism in supposing that natural science, and only natural science, tells us what there is in the world, then there seems to be no room for the existence of normative facts—or at least this will be so insofar as they cannot be reduced to the kinds of objective, causal facts with which natural science deals. Such considerations set the stage for one of the fundamental

issues confronting philosophers today: Are there any in-dispensable, irreducible normative facts involving, say, reasons, meanings, and values that are not, or cannot, be accommodated within the scientific image of the world?[16]

We will see that this last question not only divides philosophers into opposing camps; it is a key question that must be faced by anyone who seeks to defend a version of philosophical naturalism. I want to turn now to a sketch of some of the main themes in Dewey's pragmatic naturalism to provide the basis for an exploration of similarities and differences between Dewey and proponents of liberal naturalism.

2 JOHN DEWEY'S NATURALISM

In 1930, when Dewey was seventy-one, he published an autobiographical sketch titled "From Absolutism to Experimentalism."[17] He might have entitled it "From Absolutism to Naturalism." Dewey begins by reviewing his undergraduate studies at the University of Vermont. He dates his initial awakening to philosophical issues to a course in physiology that used a text by Thomas Huxley. Confessing that it is difficult to speak with exactitude about what happened to him intellectually more than fifty years ago, he nevertheless writes:

> I have an impression that there was derived from that study a sense of interdependence and interrelated unity that gave form to intellectual stirrings that had previously been inchoate, and created a kind of type or model of a view of things to which material in any field ought to conform. Subconsciously, at least, I was led to desire a world and a life that would have the same properties as had the human organism in the picture of it derived from study of Huxley's treatment.[18]

Dewey was attracted to the idea of the living organism as a model for thinking about experience and nature before he even began the formal study of philosophy. Huxley also introduced Dewey to the new biology of Darwin's theory of evolution. (Dewey was born in 1859—the year *The Origin of Species* was published.) The idea of a living, dynamic, organic-environmental interaction shaped Dewey's thinking for the rest of his life and came to full fruition in his mature naturalism. This seminal idea even influenced how he appropriated Hegelian themes.[19] In America, the 1880s and 1890s were a time of philosophical ferment; there was a strong reaction against atomistic individualism and sensationalist empiricism. Dewey shared in this ferment and was drawn to German idealism—especially the Hegelianism of his mentor at Johns Hopkins University, G.S. Morris. The philosophical themes of life, organic interaction, overcoming static dualisms that Dewey initially encountered in Huxley now found intellectual expression in his early Hegelianism. Dewey spoke of his "subjective reasons" for the appeal of Hegel and Hegelianism:

> It supplied a demand for unification that was doubtless an intense emotional craving, and yet was a hunger that only intellectualized subject-matter could satisfy. It is more than difficult, it is impossible, to recover that early mood. But the sense of divisions and separations that were, I suppose, borne in upon me as a consequence of a heritage of New England culture, divisions by way of the isolation of self from the world, of soul from body, of nature from God, brought a painful oppression—or, rather, they were an inward laceration. My earlier philosophic study had been an intellectual gymnastic. Hegel's synthesis of subject and object, matter and spirit, the divine and the human, was, however, no mere intellectual formula; it operated as an immense release, a liberation. Hegel's treatment of human culture, of institutions and the arts, involved the same dissolution of hard-and-fast dividing walls, and had a special attraction for me.[20]

The encounter with Hegel was an emotional and intellectual liberation. Throughout his career, Dewey was critical of the metaphysical and epistemological dichotomies that characterize so much of the history of philosophy. He sought to show that many of these reified dichotomies turn out to be better grasped as flexible, changing, *functional* distinctions. Dewey epitomized what he took away from Hegel when he described the Hegelianism of his mentor, G.S. Morris—a description perfectly applicable to Dewey himself:

> I should say that he was at once strangely indifferent to and strangely preoccupied with the dialectic of Hegel. Its purely technical aspects did not interest him. But he derived from it an abiding sense of what he was wont to term the organic relationship of subject and object, intelligence and the world. . . . When he talked, as he was wont to do, of the mechanical and the organic, it was this contrast which stood forth. It was a contrast between the

dead and the living, and the contrast was more moral and spiritual than physiological, though biology might afford adumbrative illustrations. His adherence to Hegel (I feel quite sure), was because Hegel demonstrated to him, in a great variety of fields of experience, the supreme reality of this principle of a living unity maintaining itself through the medium of differences and distinctions.[21]

In his early enthusiasm for Hegel, Dewey claimed that it is the dualist "Kant who does violence to science, while Hegel (I speak of his essential method and not of any particular result) is the quintessence of the scientific spirit."[22] Hegel is the quintessence of the scientific spirit because for him there is "no special, apart faculty of thought belonging to and operated by a mind existing separate from the outer world."[23]

Dewey "drifted away" from Hegel, although he admits that "acquaintance with Hegel has left a permanent deposit in . . . [his] thinking."[24] Dewey naturalized Hegel. His interest in the sciences of his day—biology, psychology, and the emerging social sciences—became much more dominant. Darwin replaced Hegel as his intellectual hero.[25] The culmination of this early phase of Dewey's development is illustrated in an important article published in 1896, "The Reflex Arc Concept in Psychology."[26] Here, Dewey works out in detail what he means by an organic-environmental interaction or coordination; he anticipates major themes of his mature theory of experience and nature.[27]

The target of Dewey's criticism is the reflex arc concept that was used by psychologists to describe and explain human behavior. Psychic behavior was taken to be a mechanical three-stage sequence: sensation or peripheral stimulus, followed by an idea or central process, followed by a motor response. Each of these moments or stages was thought to be a discrete event externally related to the other events in the arc. Dewey cites James Mark Baldwin, who claims that there are

> three elements corresponding to the three elements of the nervous arc. First, the receiving consciousness, the stimulus—say a loud, unexpected sound; second, the attention involuntarily drawn, the registering element; and third, the

muscular reaction following upon the sound—say flight from fancied danger.[28]

Dewey criticizes the reflex arc in two ways. First, the reflex arc concept *misdescribes* what actually occurs; secondly, it *distorts* what is happening. Employing the reflex arc concept in such a mechanical way ignores the prior state or set of the subject: "If one is reading a book, if one is hunting, if one is watching in a dark place on a lonely night, if one is performing a chemical experiment, in each case, the noise has a very different psychical value; it is a different experience" (RA 100). The sound is not an independent "stimulus" because the significance of the sound depends on the prior set and activity of the person experiencing the sound. Baldwin therefore reverses the actual sequence of events. The "response" is not a discrete event that follows a "stimulus." The stimulus is *constitutive* of the response insofar as the sound experience must persist as a value in the running away. And the response itself is not a totally independent event; it is the original experience, transformed and reconstituted. Stimulus and response are correlative, and the *function* of each changes in relation to the other. Consequently, just as the stimulus is constitutive of the response, the response is constitutive of the stimulus: "Just as the 'response' is necessary to constitute the stimulus, to determine it as sound and as this kind of sound, of wild beast or robber, so the sound experience must persist as a value in the running, to keep it up, to control it" (RA 102).

At first glance, it may seem that Dewey is quibbling and that he is calling for a more detailed analysis of a complex situation. His criticism cuts deeper. He argues that a unified organic-environmental coordination is the basic unit of behavior. This is a radical departure from the conception of the reflex arc as a mechanical sequence of discrete moments. The traditional reflex arc concept is a survivor of an older metaphysical dualism: it harbors the paradoxes of how mental "stuff" and physical "stuff" interact:

> The reflex arc theory . . . is a survival of the metaphysical dualism, first formulated by Plato, according to which the sensation is an ambiguous dweller on the border land of

soul and body, the idea (or central process) is purely psychical, and the act (or movement) purely physical. Thus
the reflex arc formulation is neither physical (or physiological) nor psychological; it is a mixed materialistic-
spiritualistic assumption. (RA 104)

Dewey argues that we need a new way of understanding the be-
havioral situation, where "stimulus," "central process," and
"motor response" are viewed as *functions* that play changing roles
in reconstituting a unified coordination. Dewey is not discrediting
the distinction between stimulus and response; he seeks to analyze
it properly. If we think of the reflex arc as singling out discrete
events that are entirely independent of each other, then the attempt to describe and explain human behavior is hopelessly
confused. Stimulus and response are properly understood as
changing functions; what counts as stimulus and response depends on the role it plays within an organic-environmental
coordination. Dewey summarizes this concept of an organic coordination:

The circle is a coordination, some of whose members
have come into conflict with each other. It is the temporary disintegration and need of reconstitution which
occasions, which affords the genesis of, the conscious distinction into sensory stimulus on one side and motor
response on the other. The stimulus is that phase of the
forming coordination which represents the conditions
which have to be met in bringing it to a successful issue;
the response is that phase of one and the same forming
coordination which gives the key to meeting these conditions, which serves as instrument in effecting the
successful coordination. They are therefore strictly correlative and contemporaneous. (RA 109)[29]

Dewey's analysis of organic-environmental coordination ties
together many strands in his earlier philosophic investigations and
points the way to his later theory of experience and nature. We
now have specific reasons why Dewey objects to static, mechanical
concepts: they misdescribe and distort what happens in living experience. The insights that Dewey gleaned from Hegel are

reformulated in a terminology more congenial to experimental scientific inquiry.[30] The idea of a conflict arising within an organic coordination that needs to be resolved by reconstitution or reconstruction becomes fundamental for his thinking about problem-solving. Throughout his life, Dewey criticized the atomistic and particularistic concepts of experience that had been so fundamental in the British empiricist tradition (and that had been refined by logical positivists). At the same time, Dewey rejects the tendencies in various forms of German idealism, where experience ultimately constitutes a single, all-encompassing whole. Experience, for Dewey, consists of overlapping organic-environmental coordinations. Within these coordinations, we distinguish changing functional aspects whose character is determined by the role they play in reconstituting and reconstructing the coordination. Not only is an organism transformed by its interactions with its environment, but the environment—both natural and social—is transformed through organic interactions. There is a dynamic reciprocal *dialectical* relation between an organism and its environment.[31]

In 1939, looking back over the development of his philosophy, Dewey wrote that he had attempted to formulate a *via media* between extreme atomistic pluralism and block universe monism:

> Every experience in its direct occurrence is an interaction of environing conditions and an organism. As such it contains in a fused union some*what* experienc*ed* and some processes of experienc*ing*. In its identity with a life-function, it is temporally and spatially more extensive and more internally complex than is a single thing like a stone, or a single quality like red. For no living creature could survive, save by sheer accident, if its experiences had no more reach, scope or content, than traditional particularistic empiricism provides for. On the other hand, it is impossible to imagine a living creature coping with the entire universe all at once. In other words, the theory of experiential situations which follows directly from the biological-anthropological approach is by its very nature a *via media* between extreme atomistic pluralism and block universe monisms.[32]

The concept of an organic coordination in "The Reflex Arc Concept" is one of the earliest formulations of his theory of experience that Dewey refined and elaborated throughout his life:

> Experience is primarily a process of undergoing: a process of standing something; of suffering and passion, of affection, in the literal sense of these words. The organism has to endure, to undergo, the consequences of its own actions. . . . Undergoing, however, is never mere passivity. The most patient patient is more than a receptor. He is also an agent—a reactor, one trying experiments, one concerned with undergoing in a way which may influence what is still to happen. . . . Experience, in other words, is a matter of *simultaneous* doings and sufferings.[33]

Furthermore, as Dewey emphasizes in *Experience and Nature*, "The action called 'organic' is not just that of internal structures; it is an integration of organic-environmental connections" (EN 213). We will see how this conception of experience is fundamental for the *continuity* of experience and nature. Within experience arise conflicts, tensions, and problems that call for actively experimenting and reconstructing the experience.

Robert Brandom's reflections on classical American pragmatism are illuminating for clarifying Dewey's naturalization of Hegel. The classical American pragmatists were shaped by codifying two new modes of intelligibility characteristic of nineteenth-century science. These included Darwinian evolutionary theory and the emergence of statistical scientific explanation. "Pragmatism," Brandom writes, "begins with a philosophy of science, pioneered by Peirce, that saw these two explanatory innovations as aspects of one conceptual revolution in science."[34] This conceptual shift has important philosophical consequences. The primary modality of the older mechanical physics—the modality of Newtonian laws—is *necessity*. Scientific explanation consists in showing that something is necessitated by strict universal laws. This is the way in which Kant understood the scientific explanation of natural phenomena. But in evolutionary and statistical explanations, *contingent* happenings are primary; they display conditions in which these happenings are *probable*. This conceptual

revolution is closely related to the pragmatists' doctrine of *fallibil-
ism*. Sellars epitomizes the significance of pragmatic fallibility
when he declares, "For empirical knowledge, like its sophisticated
extension, science, is rational, not because it has a *foundation* but
because it is a self-correcting enterprise which can put *any* claim in
jeopardy, though not *all* at once" (EPM 79). Brandom uses the
expression "fundamental pragmatism" to describe the basic orientation of the classical American pragmatists:

> The more specific strategy by which classical American
> pragmatists sought to naturalize the concept of *experi-
> ence*—to demystify and domesticate it, to disentangle it
> from two centuries of Cartesian encumbrances—is what
> I will call *fundamental* pragmatism. This is the idea that one
> should understand knowing *that* as a kind of knowing *how*
> (to put it in Rylean terms). That is, believing *that* things
> are thus-and-so is to be understood in terms of practical
> abilities to *do* something. Dewey, in particular, saw the
> whole philosophical tradition down to his time as perme-
> ated by a kind of platonism or intellectualism that saw a
> rule or principle, something that is or could be made con-
> ceptually or propositionally explicit, behind every bit of
> skillful practice. He contrasted that approach with the
> contrary pragmatist approach, which emphasizes the im-
> plicit context of practices and practical abilities that forms
> the necessary background against which alone states and
> performances are intelligible as explicitly contentful be-
> lievings and judgings. (PP 9)

Dewey combined this "fundamental pragmatism" with the philosophical significance of Darwinian evolutionary theory. The
primary subject matter of evolutionary explanation is, Brandom
writes, "the process by which biological species arise and diversify"
(PP 5). But Dewey, Brandom continues, generalizes this mode of
explanation by recognizing

> that *evolution*, at the level of species, and *learning*, at the
> level of individuals, share a common *selectional* structure.
> Both can be understood as processes of *adaptation*, in
> which interaction with the environment selects (preserves

and reproduces) some elements, while eliminating others. This insight is encapsulated in the concept of *habit*, and the picture of individual learning as the evolution-by-selection of a population of habits. This master idea made possible the naturalistic construal of a cognitive continuum that runs from the skillful coping of the competent predator, through the practical intelligence of primitive hominids, to the traditional practices and common sense of civilized humans, all the way to the most sophisticated theorizing of contemporary scientists. All are seen as of a piece with, intelligible in the same general terms as, biological evolution. (PP 5–6)

"Evolution," "learning," "selectional adaptation," "habit"—all become key expressions in Dewey's conception of experience and nature. The "naturalistic postulate" is fundamental for Dewey. Human beings are continuous with the rest of nature but also exhibit distinctive characteristics. Non-reductionist naturalism must do justice to both *continuity* and *difference* throughout nature but must avoid metaphysical and epistemological dualisms. Consider Dewey's claim about the "naturalistic postulate" in his *Logic: The Theory of Inquiry*:

> Any theory that rests upon a naturalistic postulate must face the problem of the extraordinary differences that mark off the activities and achievements of human beings from those of other biological forms. It is these differences that have led to the idea that man is completely separated from other animals by properties that come from a non-natural source. . . . The development of language (in its widest sense) out of prior biological activities is, in its connection with wider cultural forces, the key to this transformation. The problem, so viewed, is not the problem of the transition of organic behavior into something wholly discontinuous with it—as is the case when, for example, Reason, Intuition, and the *A priori* are appealed to for explanation of the difference. It is a special form of the general problem of continuity of change and the emergence of new modes of activity—the problem of development at any level.[35]

Dewey's pragmatic naturalism stresses continuity with difference and combines this naturalism with a thick conception of experience. Once again, Brandom's description is illuminating:

> Experience in . . . [Dewey's] sense is not the ignition of some internal Cartesian light—the occurrence of a self-initiating event of pure awareness, transparent and incorrigible to the subject of experience. Experience is *work*: the application of force through distance. It is something *done* rather than something that merely *happens*—a process, engaging in a practice, the exercise of abilities, rather than an episode. It is experience, not in the sense of *Erlebnis* (or *Empfindung*), but of Hegel's *Erfahrung*. . . . Earlier empiricists had thought of experience as the occurrence of conscious episodes that provide the raw materials for learning, via processes such as association, comparison, and abstraction. For the pragmatists, experience is not an input to the learning process. It just is learning: the process of perception and performance, followed by perception and assessment of the results of the performance, and then further performance, exhibiting the iterative, adaptive, conditional-branching structure of a test-operate-test-exit loop. The result of experience is not best thought of as the possession of items of *knowledge*, but as a kind of *understanding*, a kind of adaptive attunement to the environment, the development of habits apt for successful coping with contingencies. It is knowing how rather than knowing that. (PP 6–7)

Implicit in Brandom's account is a point that Dewey stresses over and over again: experience has a much broader significance than knowing. Following Peirce, Dewey prefers to speak about *inquiry* as a self-correcting process rather than knowing. One of Dewey's primary complaints with traditional epistemology is that it has been obsessed with experience *only* insofar as it does or does not contribute to knowledge. The epistemological obsession distorts experience as it is actually lived. Experienced organic-environmental interactions are *not* primarily cognitive or knowledge-affairs. Most of our lives consist of experiences that have little to do with knowing. Dewey frequently speaks of experiences as undergone or *had*. Experiences have distinctive qualitative characteristics that set them apart from other experiences.[36] A love affair, a memorable meal at a Michelin three-star restaurant, the grief suffered after the death of a close friend are all examples of experiences. There are pervasive qualities that distinguish these experiences from other experiences. Of course, a good deal of background knowledge may inform and shape these experiences, but this does not mean that the experiences as undergone are primarily knowledge-affairs. Experiences have both spatial and temporal dimensions. Sometimes Dewey uses the expression "situation" to designate "experience." Distinctions between what is taken to be subjective and objective are drawn *within* a situation or an experience. It is within situations or experiences that difficulties, tensions, and problems arise that call for resolution. Dewey illustrates this point when he tells us that "a variety of names serves to characterize indeterminate situations. They are disturbed, troubled, ambiguous, confused, full of conflicting tendencies, obscure, etc." (LTI 109). In Dewey's phenomenological description of experience, it is the *situation* that has these traits; they are not "merely" mental events:

> *We* are doubtful because the situation is inherently doubtful. Personal states of doubt that are not evoked by and are not relative to some existential situation are pathological; when they are extreme they constitute the mania of doubting. Consequently, situations that are disturbed and troubled, confused or obscure, cannot be straightened out, cleared up and put in order, by manipulation of our personal states of mind. . . . The habit of disposing of the doubtful as if it belonged only to *us* rather than to the existential situation in which we are caught and implicated is an inheritance from subjectivistic psychology. (LTI 109–10)[37]

In developing his pragmatic naturalism, Dewey stresses continuity within a variety of contexts. There is: (1) continuity within experience; (2) continuity between human experience and the organic-environmental interactions of nonhuman animals; (3)

continuity between commonsense inquiry and scientific inquiry; and (4) continuity between experience and nature. We have already seen that Dewey's conception of experience is not merely "mental"—consisting of discrete and separable impressions or sense data. The way in which Dewey approaches the organic-environmental interaction character of experience bears a close relation to recent ecological niche theory. Dewey also wants to restore the importance of the commonsense way in which we speak about experience when, for example, we speak of an experienced craftsman or of a memorable experience of a visit to Paris. Dewey is primarily concerned with *human* experience, but the basic idea of organic-environmental interactions is applicable to *all* living organisms.

In *Experience and Nature*, Dewey gives a rough characterization of three different emergent plateaus of natural interactions—each of which incorporates the function and relations of those below it and is such that it cannot be understood in isolation from the level (or levels) below it:

> The distinction between physical, psycho-physical, and mental is thus one of levels of increasing complexity and intimacy of interaction among natural events. The idea that matter, life and mind represent separate kinds of Being is a doctrine that springs, as so many philosophic errors have sprung, from a substantiation of eventual functions. The fallacy converts consequences of interaction of events into causes of the occurrence of these consequences—a reduplication which is significant as to the *importance* of the functions, but which hopelessly confuses understanding of them. (EN 200)

To illustrate what he means, Dewey writes, "Atoms and molecules show a selective bias in their indifferences, affinities and repulsions when exposed to other events" (EN 162). The second plateau is distinguished by "the *way* in which physico-chemical energies are interconnected and operate, whence different *consequences* mark inanimate and animate activity respectively" (EN 195). Animate bodies seek to maintain a temporal pattern of activity and to utilize consequences of past activities so as to adapt to subsequent changes to the needs of the system in which they belong. Thus,

"Iron as such exhibits characteristics of bias or selective reactions . . . . Iron as a genuine constituent of an *organized* body acts so as to tend to maintain the type of activity of the organism to which it belongs" (ibid.). The third plateau arises when the human species *begins* to develop language.[38] Dewey, who is frequently criticized for failing to take "the linguistic turn," (see, for example, PP 22, 55, 78)[39] emphasizes the emergence of language and communication in human experience. The opening of the chapter "Nature, Communication and Meaning" is poetic:

> Of all affairs, communication is the most wonderful. That things should be able to pass from the plane of external pushing and pulling to that of revealing themselves to man, and thereby to themselves; and that the fruit of communication should be participation, sharing, is a wonder by the side of which transubstantiation pales. When communication occurs, all natural events are subject to reconsideration and revision; they are re-adapted to meet the requirements of conversation, whether it be public discourse or that preliminary discourse termed thinking. (EN 132)

Although inspired by the Darwinian biological model of organic-environmental interaction, Dewey also stresses the social and cultural dimensions of human life:

> Man, as Aristotle remarked, is a *social* animal. This fact introduces him into situations and originates problems and ways of solving them that have no precedent upon the organic biological level. For man is social in another sense than the bee and ant, since his activities are encompassed in an environment that is culturally transmitted, so that what man does and how he acts, is determined not by organic structure and physical heredity alone but by the influence of cultural heredity, embedded in traditions, institutions, customs and the purposes and beliefs they both carry and inspire. (LTI 49)

Dewey stresses the importance of language and communication in characterizing human experience, but he is deeply skeptical about the traditional dichotomy of mind and body. In Dewey's naturalism,

> there is no breach of continuity between operations of
> inquiry and biological operations and physical operations.
> "Continuity" . . . means that rational operations *grow out*
> of organic activities, without being identical with that
> from which they emerge. (LTI 26)

Mind, for him, is always *embodied*. He coins the awkward expression of "body-mind" to emphasize this embodiment:

> Body-mind simply designates what actually takes place
> when a living body is implicated in situations of discourse,
> communication and participation. In the hyphenated
> phrase body-mind, "body" designates the continued and
> conserved, the registered and cumulative operation of
> factors continuous with the rest of nature, inanimate as
> well as animate; while "mind" designates the characters
> and consequences which are differential, indicative of fea-
> tures which merge when "body" is engaged in a wider,
> more complex and interdependent situation. (EN 217)

Mark Johnson, in a succinct summary of Dewey's conception of
embodied mind, writes:

> We can appropriately speak of mind whenever our en-
> gagement with our environment involves capacities for
> recognizing patterns, marking distinctions, and coordinat-
> ing behaviors by means of symbolic interactions. Mind is
> an evolutionary accomplishment that cannot exist with-
> out a body in continual interaction with its world. Thus,
> for Dewey, mind is not an innate capacity or a distinct
> metaphysical entity or substance. Rather, mind emerges
> out of the strivings of certain highly developed organisms
> who have learned to inquire, communicate, and coordi-
> nate their activities through the use of symbols. Mind is
> the primary vehicle by which creatures like us are able to
> sustain our existence, pursue our various conceptions of
> well-being, share meaning, and engage in the distinctive
> forms of inquiry that mark our species.[40]

Dewey is fully aware that when he distinguishes the three
emerging evolutionary plateaus, he is giving a *rough* characterization of these plateaus. When we ask for specific descriptions and

explanations of how inanimate natural interactions give rise to animate and human interactions, we have to turn to specific developments in scientific inquiries. Philosophical reflection, however, can criticize the appeal to metaphysical and epistemological dichotomies to account for these different plateaus and for the emergence of distinctive human capacities. Philosophical reflection must always be open to what we learn from scientific inquiry. This is fundamental for Dewey's pragmatic naturalism. Dewey was also critical of the quest for certainty and the spectator theory of knowing. The only certainty we achieve is a *practical* certainty that is, in principle, open to critical revision. And we never achieve a position *outside* language and the world where we can view the world *sub specie æternitatis*. The philosophical task is never finally completed; it must be performed over and over again in light of what we learn from novel forms of scientific inquiry. In this respect, Dewey departs from another philosophical tradition: the attempt to define philosophy in such a manner that it is immune to what we learn from experimental, empirical science. He objects to the very idea of transcendental philosophy as a pure discipline that is isolated from what we learn from scientific inquiry. He would be just as critical of those contemporary philosophers who draw a *fixed* distinction between conceptual analysis and empirical inquiry.[41] Dewey is certainly not denying that there are distinctive issues, concerns, and aims of philosophical reflection—and these change over time. But philosophical inquiry is continuous with scientific inquiry in the sense that it must always be prepared to learn from new scientific developments. This does not mean that philosophy is a "placeholder" that will eventually be replaced by one or a combination of the natural sciences. Dewey drew on the sciences of his time, but he would insist that as new scientific inquiries emerge, naturalism itself has to be rethought. Dewey would endorse Rouse's conception of naturalism as a "historically situated philosophical project" that must always be prepared to meet new challenges (AW 6). He takes seriously the Peircean principle: Do not block the way of inquiry![42]

The most contentious area where Dewey's claims about continuity have been challenged concerns the continuity between experience and nature. During his lifetime, Dewey was frequently accused of being anthropocentric—of taking human experience as primary and projecting its categories onto the rest of nature— even though he declared that "experience is *of* as well as *in* nature. It is not experience that is experienced, but nature—stones, plants, animals, diseases, health, temperature, electricity, and so on. Things interacting in certain ways *are* experience; they are what is experienced" (EN 12). There is no doubt that Dewey was primarily concerned with *human* experience. He was deeply motivated by ethical, political, and social concerns—with enabling human beings to enlighten and enrich their experiences, with reconstructing experience so that it is funded with intelligence.

Cohen, a fellow American naturalist, claimed that Dewey was anthropocentric in the *pejorative* sense—that he showed no interest in what nature is like before the emergence of human beings. For Cohen, experience is something that happens only with humans; experience is only one type of natural event—it cannot be used to describe all of nature.[43] Sinclair summarizes Cohen's most important objections:

> Cohen emphasizes that if our understanding of the universe is not to remain completely subjective but be determined through objective consequences, then it cannot be exhausted in the thoughts, and emotions of human beings. Dewey's anthropocentric naturalism then attaches too much significance to human categories when describing nature, and as a result fails to maintain the vital distinctions between human nature and non-human nature, and between subjective human experience, and the objective nature of the things experienced. Without them, a proper conception of naturalism cannot be formulated.[44]

Cohen is clearly right about one key point: the sciences that most interested Dewey were biology, psychology, anthropology, and the emerging social sciences. He showed little interest in the physical sciences, mathematics, or formal logic. But the key question is if Cohen is correct in claiming that Dewey cannot formulate a "proper conception of naturalism."

Let us consider how Dewey responds to Cohen. It is a truism that it is only by human inquiry that we come to know about nature—whether it is human or nonhuman. All inquiry arises from the problems that emerge out of human organic-environmental interactions. But this does not mean that human beings are *projecting* their "subjective" categories onto nature. On the contrary, the point of disciplined inquiry is to distinguish what is merely subjective from what can be objectively warranted. There are no intrinsic limits on what we can come to know about nature by scientific human inquiry. From Dewey's perspective, Cohen is confusing the *methodological* character of human inquiry with the *warranted results* of inquiry—what we learn about nature when inquiry is carried out in a disciplined manner.

There is a type of circularity between experience and nature, but it is not a vicious circularity: "Analysis and interpretation of nature is made dependent upon the conclusions of the natural sciences, especially upon biology, but upon a biology that is itself dependent upon physics and chemistry."[45] To say that knowledge of nature is dependent on what we learn from the natural sciences does not mean that the

> material of experienced things *qua* experienced must be translated into the terms of the material of the physical sciences; that view leads to a naturalism which denies distinctive significance to experience, thereby ending in the identification of naturalism with mechanistic materialism.[46]

Dewey continues,

> If we look at human history and especially at the historical development of the natural sciences, we find progress made from a crude experience in which beliefs about nature and natural events were very different from those now scientifically authorized. At the same time we find the latter now enable us to frame a theory of experience by which we can tell *how* this development out of gross experience into the highly refined conclusions of science has taken place.[47]

In short—and to repeat—, approaching human inquiry as arising within the context of organic-environmental interactions does not place any intrinsic limitations on what we can come to know—whether it be the knowledge of geological ages that long preceded the emergence of animate life or the natural conditions in which animate and human life arises. But Dewey argues that on the basis of what we have already learned from the sciences—especially as a result of evolutionary theory—we can *begin* to understand how human experience has emerged from nonhuman natural interactions. I emphasize "begin" because there are still many difficult scientific issues that need to be solved to provide detailed answers to how human experience emerges in evolutionary history. When Dewey insists upon the continuity of experience and nature, he is not prejudging what we have yet to learn and will learn from scientific inquiry. Rather, he stresses that there are distinctive features of human experience that distinguish it from other natural interactions.[48]

I have presented this brief sketch of Dewey's naturalism because I want to explore its relation to more contemporary versions of naturalism. There are many questions that can be raised about both Dewey's general claims and the details of his discussion. I want, however, to consider one major criticism by Brandom. This will provide a transition to the discussion of contemporary liberal naturalisms.

Brandom combines his sympathetic discussion of classical American pragmatism with some very sharp criticisms. He objects to what he takes to be Dewey's "instrumental pragmatism."[49] He also thinks—along with Rorty—that the classical American pragmatists failed to take "the linguistic turn."[50] They failed to put "language at the center of philosophical concerns and [understand] philosophical problems . . . in terms of the language one uses in formulating them" (PP 22). Brandom's primary—and potentially devastating—objection is that Dewey's claims about continuity blur the sharp differences between human *sapient* linguistic creatures and nonhuman *sentient* creatures. Although Dewey acknowledges the importance of human language and communication, he fails to clearly *demarcate* the differences that arise when human beings master language—especially discursive propositional language. Dewey fails to answer the questions: "What is distinctive of linguistic (or discursive) practices? What sets them apart from prelinguistic or nondiscursive practices?" (PP 28). Brandom's own linguistic, rationalistic pragmatism can be viewed as a sustained and systematic attempt to answer these questions. The key for answering the demarcation question is to acknowledge the distinctive *normativity* of our discursive practices:

> My idea is that pragmatism can usefully be combined with a *rationalist* criterion of demarcation of the linguistic—and hence of discursiveness in general. By this I mean that what distinguishes the linguistic practice in virtue of which we are sapient and not merely sentient beings is its core practices of giving and asking for *reasons*. (PP 29–30)

After enumerating the many ways in which classical American pragmatists were progressive, Brandom claims that they did not share "the distinctively twentieth-century philosophical concern with *language*, and with the *dis*continuities with nature that it establishes and enforces" (PP 55).[51] Dewey, Brandom argues, is guilty of "naturalistic assimilationism" (PP 55).[52] Brandom grants "that even now we have not yet sorted out the tensions between naturalistic assimilationism and the normative exceptionalism about the discursive practices most distinctive of us" (PP 55). But he thinks that the "way forward from the ideas of the American pragmatists must be a *linguistic* pragmatism" (ibid.).

When Brandom speaks of "normative exceptionalism," we hear the echoes of the problem raised by De Caro and Macarthur when they discussed naturalism and normativity. Reaching back further (as Brandom does), we hear Kant in the background—the Kant who sharply distinguishes the normative character of reason and contrasts it with nature, a nature that is known by the natural sciences. The most immediate predecessor of, and a major influence on, Brandom is Sellars, especially Sellars's explication of the normative, social, linguistic character of our conceptual capacities. Sellars's *Empiricism and the Philosophy of Mind* has inspired a whole tradition of "left Sellarsians," which includes Rorty, Brandom, and McDowell, among others. They endorse Sellars's critique of the myth of the given; his critique of traditional empiricism, phenomenalism, and logical positivism; his antifoundationalism; his distinction between natural causation and epistemological justification; his "psychological nominalism"; and, especially, his famous claim that

> in characterizing an episode or a state as that of *knowing*, we are not giving an empirical description of that episode or state; we are placing it in the logical space of reasons, of justifying and being able to justify what one says. (EPM 76).[53]

Neither the concepts of experience nor naturalism play any significant role in Brandom's linguistic, rationalistic pragmatism, but both concepts are central for McDowell.[54] McDowell was one of the first contemporary philosophers to use the expression "liberal naturalism" to name the type of naturalism that he defends. By examining his conception(s) of naturalism, we will have a basis for exploring how they are related to Dewey's naturalism.

3 LIBERAL NATURALISM(S)

In "Naturalism in the Philosophy of Mind," McDowell shows how a distinction arises between a common, modern understanding of nature and the justificatory practices of the logical space of reasons. He writes that

> on a familiar modern understanding of nature, a contrast opens between saying how something is placed in the space of reasons—a logical space that is organized by justificatory relations between its inhabitants—and saying how something is placed in nature. The contrast is such as to suggest that the content of concepts that belong in the space of reasons, such as the concept of knowledge, cannot be captured in terms of the concepts that belong in the contrasting logical space, the space of placement in nature.[55]

It is not difficult to hear the Kantian overtones of the contrast that McDowell is drawing. The conception of nature that lies at the basis of this contrast is one that has its origins in the rise of modern science. This is the conception of nature that McDowell, following Max Weber, characterizes as "disenchanted" in *Mind and World*—where meaning is expelled from nature, and we conceive of nature as "the realm of law."[56] "Bald naturalism," an expression that McDowell coined (MW xviii–ix), claims that what Kant and Kantians call "spontaneity" (MW 4) can be adequately accounted for by the natural sciences. The most straightforward version of bald naturalism is reductionism, but there are other varieties (MW 73). McDowell is skeptical of all versions of bald naturalism.[57] Although Dewey does not use the term "bald naturalism," he clearly rejects this version of naturalism. (Dewey—similar to many of McDowell's critics—questions whether this conception of nature as "the realm of law" is actually presupposed or endorsed by modern science.[58]) McDowell—unlike bald naturalists—does think that the contrast between the realm of natural law and the space of reasons is *genuine*: "The structure of the space of reasons stubbornly resists being appropriated within a naturalism that conceives nature as the realm of law" (MW 73). One might think that McDowell identifies himself with those interpreters of Kant who maintain that there is a strict dichotomy between nature and reason. But this is not the position that McDowell advocates. McDowell is not calling into question the achievements of modern science, but he is calling into question whether the "disenchanted" conception of nature is an *adequate* conception of nature—especially of human nature:

> Even though the logical space that is the home of the idea of spontaneity cannot be aligned with the logical space that is the home of ideas of what is natural in the relevant sense, conceptual powers are nevertheless operative in the workings of our sensibility, in actualizations of our *animal nature*, as such. (MW 74; emphasis added)

This last phrase provides the essential clue for McDowell's version of liberal naturalism. Although spontaneity—the source of our conceptual powers—is *sui generis*, it is not unnatural or supernatural (see esp. MW 74–6). It is integral to our nature as human animals. In *Mind and World*, McDowell elaborates this enlarged conception of nature by an appeal to Aristotle—especially Aristotle's ethics (see MW 78). In order to elaborate an adequate conception of nature, we need to blend Kantian and Aristotelian insights:

> We need to recapture the Aristotelian idea that a normal mature human being is a rational animal, but without losing the Kantian idea that rationality operates freely in its own sphere. The Kantian idea is reflected in the contrast between the organization of the space of reasons and the structure of the realm of natural law. Modern naturalism is forgetful of second nature; if we try to preserve the Kantian thought that reason is autonomous within the framework of that kind of naturalism, we disconnect our rationality from our animal being, which is what gives us our foothold in nature. The upshot is a temptation to drop the Kantian thought and naturalize our rationality in

the manner of bald naturalism. . . . *We need to see ourselves as animals whose natural being is permeated with rationality, even though rationality is appropriately conceived in Kantian terms.* (MW 85; emphasis added)

This enlarged naturalism, which combines Aristotelian and Kantian insights, McDowell calls "liberal naturalism." "Restrictive" or "bald naturalism" is sharply contrasted with liberal naturalism:

The first approach—a restrictive naturalism—aims to naturalize the concepts of thinking and knowing by forcing the conceptual structure in which they belong into the framework of the realm of law. This second approach—a liberal naturalism—does not accept that to reveal thinking and knowing as natural, we need to integrate into the realm of law the frame within which the concepts of thinking and knowing function. All we need is to stress that they are concepts of occurrences and states in our lives.[59]

How does McDowell's version of liberal naturalism relate to Dewey's naturalism?[60] Although the idioms are strikingly different, and McDowell takes account of the significant contemporary contributions of Sellars, Gareth Evans, Donald Davidson, Rorty, Wittgenstein, and others, there is a great deal of *substantive* overlap. As mentioned above, Dewey is also critical of what McDowell calls "bald" or "restrictive naturalism."[61] However, unlike McDowell, Dewey does not look at Kant as one of his heroes. Dewey reads Kant as Hegel did—as a philosopher committed to unstable dualisms, including the dualism of reason and nature.[62] McDowell himself, influenced by Hegel's criticisms of Kant, rejects this dualistic interpretation of Kant (see esp. MW 44, 83, 111). The rationale for McDowell's appeal to the Aristotelian concept of second nature is to show that we can *naturalize* Kant. Dewey would claim that this naturalization of Kant is already implicit in Hegel, who self-consciously sought to reconcile Kant and Aristotle.[63]

What about McDowell's insistence that Kantian spontaneity is *sui generis*? This is certainly not Dewey's language. McDowell is aware that speaking in this manner lends itself to an interpretation of a "Platonic," supernatural conception of reason. He labels such a *supernatural* conception of reason "rampant Platonism" (MW 77–8). This is precisely what his liberal naturalism is intended to *avoid*. McDowell, like Dewey, seeks to avoid any concession to supernaturalism—including appealing to a supernatural (Platonic) faculty of reason:[64]

> To avoid conceiving thinking and knowing as supernatural, we should stress that thinking and knowing are aspects of our lives. The concept of a life is the concept of the career of a living thing, and hence obviously the concept of something natural. But there are aspects of our lives whose description requires concepts that function in the space of reasons. We are rational animals. . . . *Thinking and knowing are part of our way of being animals.*[65]

Dewey prefers to speak of "intelligence" rather than "reason," because "reason" has so often been thought of as a non-natural or supernatural concept. But otherwise he would completely endorse McDowell's claim that thinking and knowing are not supernatural but are aspects of our natural lives.

Still, one might want to contrast Dewey's emphasis on *continuity* with McDowell's insistence on the *sui generis* character of the logical space of reasons. We should recall that Dewey affirms the "extraordinary differences" that distinguish the achievements of human beings, who have mastered linguistic communication, from other biological forms (LTI 49).[66] Dewey, like McDowell and other left Sellarsians, associates these extraordinary differences with the achievement of human language. Given the sophistication of what has been achieved in analytic philosophy, McDowell is able to articulate our conceptual capacities in a much more fine-grained manner. But I am not convinced that there is significant substantive disagreement between Dewey's claim about the "extraordinary differences" that result from the emergence of human language and McDowell's claims about the *sui generis* character of spontaneity. Concerning the emergence of language, Dewey writes:

> Language grew out of unintelligent babblings . . . . But nevertheless language once called into existence is language and operates as language. It operates not to perpetuate the forces which produced it but to modify

and redirect them. . . . What is said of the institution of
language holds good of every institution. . . . These are
not mere embellishments of the forces which produced
them, idle decorations of the scene. They are additional
forces. . . . They open new avenues of endeavor and im-
pose new labors.[67]

Just as McDowell denies that there is a *gap* between nature and
(conceptual) norms, so does Dewey. Dewey would completely endorse McDowell's claim that "modern philosophy has taken itself
to be called on to bridge dualistic gulfs, between subject and object, thought and world. This style of approach to meaning sets
out to bridge a dualism of norm and nature" (MW 93). McDowell
questions these dualisms—including the "deeper dualism" of nature and norm (ibid.)—and so does Dewey. Dewey would also
agree with McDowell when the latter affirms "that philosophy
must not be allowed to make a mystery out of thought's bearing
on its objects" (MW 138).

We will see, however, that there are major differences between
Dewey and McDowell that turn out to be to Dewey's advantage.
These differences are already indicated in a key passage from *Mind
and World*, where McDowell says that once we grasp the naturalism
of second nature, then no further constructive philosophy is
needed:

The naturalism of second nature that I have been describing is precisely a shape for our thinking that would leave
even the last dualism [the dualism of norms and nature]
not seeming to call for constructive philosophy. The bare
idea of *Bildung* ensures that the autonomy of meaning is
not inhuman, and that should eliminate the tendency to
be spooked by the very idea of norms or demands of reason. This leaves no genuine questions about norms, apart
from those that we address in reflective thinking about
specific norms, an activity that is not particularly philosophical. *There is no need for constructive philosophy*, directed at
the very idea of norms of reason, or the structure within
which meaning comes into view, from the standpoint of
the naturalism that threatens to disenchant nature. (MW
94–5; emphasis added)

McDowell thinks that a major source of anxieties and obsessions of modern philosophy arises from the assumption that the concept of nature presupposed and endorsed by modern science provides an adequate concept of nature. When this blind spot is removed, and we accept a liberal naturalism that acknowledges our second nature, then the anxieties generated by modern philosophy are presumably dissipated. These philosophical anxieties are groundless. Once we dispel these anxieties and obsessions, our philosophical work is finished. This has been called McDowell's "quietism," where the primary task of philosophy is therapeutic, namely to uncover and reveal the misleading presuppositions and dualisms that are the source of philosophical anxieties and thereby to dissipate these anxieties.[68]

Several of McDowell's contemporaries have been extremely critical of this quietism, including Rouse and Godfrey-Smith. They raise criticisms of McDowell that are very much in the spirit of Dewey. Rouse points out that McDowell does not think that any "constructive philosophical or scientific work is needed to grasp how conceptual capacities, including capacities for scientific understanding, are compatible with a scientific understanding of nature" (AW 12). For McDowell, "Only misguided philosophical anxieties could drive further inquiry into *how* rational spontaneity is grounded in human biological potentialities" (ibid.). Rouse affirms—as Dewey would—that "McDowell is right that our received conceptions of nature and science foreclose a more thoroughly naturalistic incorporation of scientific understanding within nature as scientifically understood" (AW 13). But unlike McDowell, Rouse asserts that this conceptual impasse calls for renewed philosophical reflection and scientific inquiry, rather than acquiescence: "Such reflection and inquiry should also aspire to advance our self-understanding constructively and not merely to relieve recurrent philosophical anxieties about our conceptual footing in the world" (ibid.). Dewey would clearly agree with Rouse.[69]

While Rouse does not refer to Dewey, Godfrey-Smith explicitly criticizes McDowell from a Deweyan perspective. He also champions the case for Dewey's contemporary relevance. Godfrey-

Smith reminds us that McDowell's understanding of second nature is intended to be "a description of *our* second nature, a
description of a set of skills and habits that are natural to properly
enculturated humans."[70] Like Rouse (and Dewey), Godfrey-Smith
argues for the viability and importance of an investigation that
McDowell resists. Even if we accept McDowell's description of
second nature and *Bildung*, there are still important philosophical
and scientific questions to be addressed constructively.[71] What are
the set of habits and skills that constitute second nature?[72] "What
sort of coordination does . . . [second nature] give us with one
another and with the world at large?"[73] McDowell thinks he can
dismiss such questions because they take what he calls a "sideways-on" perspective toward our second nature (MW 34–6).[74] But
what grounds does McDowell have to resist and dismiss such
questions? Raising these questions does not entail falling back on
familiar gulf-bridging projects of modern philosophy. It can be
carried out with the type of naturalism that we find in Dewey—a
naturalism that emphasizes continuity rather than dualisms.
McDowell clearly objects to a form of naturalism that he associates with "the realm of law." But as Godfrey-Smith rightly notes,
many naturalists, including Dewey, "would deny that laws are central to the scientific outlook, either in general or in the context of
understanding human capacities."[75] The real weak spot in
McDowell's quietism is his aversion to the theoretical investigation
of second nature. McDowell aims to deter, for example, the following kind of inquiry:

> Suppose we have a philosopher [like Dewey] who has
> taken full heed of the missteps in the tradition, especially
> the erecting of boundaries between thought and nature,
> also someone who does not think of science as obsessed
> with locking events into laws. What the philosopher wants
> to do is ask general questions about how the "habits of
> thought and action" involved in our use of normative
> concepts relate to other facts about us and how these hab-
> its function as human cognitive tools. When this
> philosopher says that such an investigation should mesh
> with what we learn from science, do not think "physics"

when he says "science." Instead, think social psychology, a field that overflows with the most startling results almost untapped by philosophy. Think comparative psychology, which has recently become intensely concerned with the ways in which various nonhuman animals have *partial* analogues of the key human characteristic of cultural learning and is intensely concerned with how and why the human lineage took an extra step.[76]

Dewey would fully endorse Godfrey-Smith's claim about taking account of what we learn from the sciences—especially the sciences closely related to the study of human beings.

Godfrey-Smith's Deweyan criticism of McDowell underscores a more general critique. McDowell asserts over and over again that modern science is committed to an understanding of nature in the framework of "the realm of law." But what is the basis for this global claim? There is something deeply disturbing—a hidden essentialism—in characterizing modern science as if it were a single unified discipline. McDowell does not attempt to justify his claim by analyzing what actually takes place in the different sciences. Philosophers of science such as John Dupré and Nancy Cartwright, who engage in detailed investigation of actual sciences, call into question the very idea of something called "modern science."[77] There is enormous diversity among the sciences, including the natural sciences. It is a misleading myth to speak of "modern science" as if it were a *single* discipline committed to a *single* conception of nature. Despite his objections to naturalistic reductionism, McDowell appears to be committed to a different type of reductionism whereby all of modern science can be reduced to "the realm of law." Although McDowell is concerned with human nature, he never really takes into account how evolutionary theory—either in its classical Darwinian form or in contemporary revisions—contributes to our understanding of human beings, including their linguistic abilities, thinking, and knowing. Nor does he take any account of the relevance of the ecological sciences for understanding human beings. Even if we grant that all natural sciences are ultimately dependent on physics and chemistry (as Dewey does), it is a gross simplification to classify evolutionary theory and all the sciences concerned with animate creatures as existing in a framework of "the realm of law."[78]

There is also something troubling about the way in which McDowell and other left Sellarsians understand concepts. For McDowell, what is properly taken to be conceptual must be something that *can* be taken up in a judgment (or a proposition).[79] The inspiration for this way of thinking is clearly Kant—and the Kantianism of Sellars. The idea that human beings have conceptual capacities, are able to make judgments and inferences, and have the capacity to justify claims is not controversial. To claim, as McDowell does, that "dumb animals do not have Kantian freedom" is a truism (MW 182). Who would deny this?[80] Much of the philosophical thinking inspired by Kant and Sellars has been concerned with clarifying the meaning and role of conceptual capacities, judgments, and inferences—i.e., with the type of *discourse* where we can advance, justify, and criticize reasons. But there is a danger that this preoccupation focuses *exclusively* on how humans operate with concepts in making and justifying judgments. If this becomes the paradigm of what is "genuinely" conceptual, then we are compelled to say that nonhuman animals do not, "strictly speaking," have conceptual capacities because they do not have the ability to make and justify judgments; they do not have Kantian spontaneity.[81] We are sapient and they (nonhuman animals) are *only* sentient. But this obsession with the "logical space of reasons" tends to make us insensitive to the continuities between nonhuman and human animals.[82] It closes us off to the possibility of learning more about our conceptual capacities by studying how these are anticipated in nonhuman animals, especially those "higher" creatures who are close to us in evolutionary development.[83]

McDowell's conceptualism is *not* based on empirical investigation of animals—either human or nonhuman. Rather, given his understanding of concepts, it is an *a priori* truth implicit in his understanding of what is "truly" conceptual—conceptual in the "demanding sense," as McDowell often puts it (see MW 47, 63, 69–70, 121). Consequently, it does not need any empirical defense.

For him, the conceptual is unbounded, which means that every-
thing that we consciously apprehend—including our intuitions
and perceptions—is saturated with concepts.[84] Kantian spontaneity, for McDowell, is an all-or-nothing affair. One does not have
to deny that there is something distinctive about the way in which
human beings exercise their higher conceptual capacities and make
judgments. But there is no room in McDowell's conceptualism for
seeing how some of the remarkable things that nonhuman animals
can do may help to illuminate *degrees* and *gradations* in acquiring
Kantian spontaneity.[85] McDowell is not denying that we can learn
a great deal from evolutionary theory and other sciences about
animals—both human and nonhuman—, but he seems to think
that these sciences cannot illuminate what is distinctive about
Kantian spontaneity.

There are many philosophers today who are not reductionists
and who are not wedded to traditional metaphysical and epistemological dualisms. Philosophers like Godfrey-Smith, Kitcher,
Jennifer Welchman, Rouse, Ruth Millikan, and Daniel Dennett argue that we can learn a great deal about our conceptual abilities
from the natural sciences, especially evolutionary theory. In effect,
they, like Dewey, argue for a more dialectical relationship between
philosophical conceptual analysis and empirical scientific inquiry.[86]
Despite McDowell's aversion to philosophical dualisms, his conceptualism reinforces a rigid dichotomy between human beings
and "dumb animals" (see MW 69–70).[87] McDowell tells us that
thinking is *embodied*, but he is not seriously interested in exploring
the character of embodied mind. He seems to think that when he
introduces the concepts of second nature and *Bildung*, nothing more
needs to be said about how *Bildung* is embodied and cultivated (see,
for example, MW 125). Dewey's insistence on breaking down the
dualism of body and mind is intended to illuminate what is involved
in the embodied mind. Johnson summarizes Dewey's view:

> Dewey founds his theory of mind and thought on the as-
> sumption that a human being is a living organism, with at
> least a mostly functioning brain and body, engaged in con-
> tinuous interaction with various environments, which are

at once physical, social, and cultural. Mind has deep biological dimensions, but is also fundamentally a social
phenomenon. . . . Dewey attempts to explain "mind" and
all its operations and activities nondualistically, as
grounded in bodily operations of living human creatures,
who are themselves the result of prior evolutionary history and who have typically passed through a crucial
sequence of developmental stages that have shaped their
cognitive capacities and their identity.[88]

I want to say something more about Godfrey-Smith's Deweyan
pragmatic naturalism—a pragmatic naturalism that takes account
of recent scientific developments as well as debates within contemporary analytic philosophy. Godfrey-Smith has made
important contributions to philosophy of science, philosophy of
biology, epistemology, and philosophy of mind. Unlike many of
his Anglophone colleagues, he has emphasized the importance
and relevance of Dewey. Godfrey-Smith thinks that *"Experience
and Nature* is—despite its excesses, its endless repetition, its occa-
sional incomprehensibility—the best book written in the
pragmatist lineage so far."[89] Unlike Rorty, he stresses the relevance
of Dewey for understanding metaphysical and epistemological
themes.[90] He seeks to show how Dewey can be related not only to
contemporary discussions of naturalism but also to disputes about
realism and science.[91]

I think Dewey would be enthusiastic about Godfrey-Smith's
popular book, *Other Minds: The Octopus, the Sea, and the Deep Origins
of Consciousness*—especially his discussion of evolutionary theory.[92]
Godfrey-Smith's passionate interest in octopuses is informed by
his personal observations, his sophisticated reflections on the latest developments in the evolution of cephalopods, and the
scientific investigation of the (relatively) large brains of octopuses.
He gives a clear account of what is scientifically well established,
what is still contested, and what is still unknown. A fallibilistic
spirit pervades his inquiry, especially when he seeks to distinguish
a more "primitive" form of subjective experience from what we
call "consciousness."[93] Godfrey-Smith contrasts our minds with
the alien octopus minds.[94] The reason I think that Dewey would

admire this book is because of Godfrey-Smith's methodological approach. Godfrey-Smith's philosophical hypotheses are always informed by an understanding of the latest relevant scientific research and experiments. Contrast his sophisticated appropriation of scientific experimental inquiries with McDowell's "arm-chair" approach. McDowell rarely refers to concrete scientific research and prefers to make generalized claims about "modern science" and "the realm of law." One can well understand why Dewey is one of Godfrey- Smith's heroes, because the latter's scientifically informed naturalism is a genuine successor to Dewey's naturalistic orientation. Despite McDowell's advocacy of liberal naturalism, I suspect that Dewey would claim that an unintended consequence of McDowell's mode of philosophizing is to reify a dichotomy between conceptual (transcendental?) analysis and experimental, empirical inquiries. A major reason for Dewey's insistence on continuity is to challenge this dichotomy—one that blocks us from being open to what we can learn about human beings from scientific inquiries. Such an open approach is fully compatible with the acknowledgment that the "higher" conceptual capacities of human beings are distinctive and even, in an appropriate sense, *sui generis*.

To develop further my thesis about the legacy of Dewey's pragmatic naturalism, I also want to consider Kitcher's contributions to a pragmatic reconstruction of philosophy. Kitcher, like Rorty, Putnam, and Godfrey-Smith, has had a similar trajectory in his philosophical career. All four achieved prominence and recognition for their contributions to one or more areas of analytic philosophy. Although they have mastered the argumentative techniques of analytic philosophy, each became increasingly discontented with the narrowness of professional technical philosophy. In their search for a broader philosophical canvas, they turned to classical American pragmatism, especially to the works of Dewey. Each has stressed different aspects of Dewey. Godfrey-Smith and Putnam—unlike Rorty—have focused on the ways in which Dewey contributes to new perspectives on science, realism, and naturalism. Kitcher places greater emphasis on the way in which Dewey (and James) call for a reconstruction of philosophy.[95] Like Rorty, Kitcher is extremely critical of the exaggerated pretentions of technical academic philosophy.[96] He is inspired by Dewey's vision of a synthetic philosophy that draws widely from many areas of human inquiry.[97] Like Dewey, Kitcher calls for philosophers to employ their analytic skills to deal with those problems that have real significance for human beings and to break out of the vicious circle where philosophers deal with technical issues that can be appreciated only by fellow philosophers interested in the same narrow issues.[98]

Kitcher's collection of articles entitled *Preludes to Pragmatism* has the Deweyan subtitle, "Toward a Reconstruction of Philosophy." Kitcher wants to carry out Dewey's project of reforming and reconstructing philosophy for *our* time, dealing with some of the most serious problems that we now confront, such as climate change and the role of religion in our public lives. His introduction to the *Preludes* is entitled "From Naturalism to Pragmatic Naturalism," and traces his own philosophic development. Here, Kitcher articulates and defends a nonscientistic liberal naturalism:

> Naturalism of this sort will be at odds with the frequent philosophical practice of casual positing, and its suspicions will be expressed in resistance to Platonic Forms, Aristotelian essences, processes of Pure Reason, claims that favorite premises are *a priori* truths, intuitions of the Good, and a host of other less prominent denizens of the philosophical zoo.[99]

Kitcher stresses that Dewey's naturalism is not primarily intended to be another system to compete with traditional metaphysical and epistemological systems but rather to serve as the basis for developing a conception of experience and nature that will enable ordinary human beings to enlighten and enrich their social, ethical, political, aesthetic, and even their religious experiences.[100] Kitcher endorses Dewey's famous claim from *Democracy and Education* that "philosophy may even be defined *as the general theory of education*."[101] When Kitcher turns explicitly to the discussion of "Deweyan Naturalism," he introduces a distinction between the "content naturalist" and "method naturalist." Content naturalists "turn to the content of various areas of natural science in search of insights for the reform of philosophy."[102] Dewey's "method naturalism" is not of this type; his "guiding idea in campaigning for a naturalistic renewal of philosophy looks to the ways of proceeding that he identifies as crucial to the success of the natural sciences."[103]

Kitcher's distinction between "content" and "method naturalism" at once directs us back to Dewey's debate with Cohen and forward to Price's distinction between "object naturalism" and "subject naturalism." Recall that Cohen criticized Dewey for being anthropocentric and for failing to pay much attention to the nature that is revealed by those natural sciences that do not deal directly with human beings. Dewey replied that a proper understanding of human experience and inquiry shows that there are no *a priori* limits to what the sciences can potentially teach us about human and nonhuman nature. When Dewey appeals to the sciences, he primarily focuses his attention on the need for philosophy to incorporate the fallibilistic, self-corrective *practices* of science into its own procedures.

Price also seeks to articulate a pragmatic naturalism that focuses on the practices of human beings. This is what he calls "subject naturalism," which he distinguishes from "object naturalism."[104] Object naturalism exists in both ontological and epistemological keys: "As an ontological doctrine, it is the view that in some important sense, all there *is* is in the world studied by science. As an epistemological doctrine, it is the view that all genuine knowledge is scientific knowledge."[105] (If we interpret Sellars's famous statement about science being the measure of all that *is* in a straightforward manner, then Sellars's naturalism is a paradigmatic version of object naturalism [EPM 83]. In his analysis of the scientific image, he focuses his attention on its *primary objects*.) Object naturalism "implies that in so far as philosophy is concerned with the nature of objects and properties of various kinds, its concern is with something in the natural world, or with nothing at all. For there simply is nothing else" (NWR 5). Subject naturalism insists that "philosophy needs to begin with what science tells us *about ourselves*. Science tells us that we humans are natural creatures, and if the claims and ambitions of philosophy conflict with this view, then philosophy needs to give way" (ibid.).[106]

Initially, it might seem that subject naturalism is a corollary of object naturalism. This is the view that Cohen pressed against Dewey and is the view held today by many who call themselves naturalists. But Price's striking thesis is that subject naturalism is not a derivative form of object naturalism. Subject naturalism comes first; it has *priority* over object naturalism. Price sums up his claims in two theses:

> **Priority Thesis** Subject naturalism is theoretically prior to object naturalism, because the latter depends on validation from a subject naturalist perspective.

> **Invalidity Thesis** There are strong reasons for doubting whether object naturalism deserves to be "validated"— whether its presuppositions do survive subject naturalist scrutiny. (NWR 6)

To flesh out what is at issue in these two views of naturalism, we need to pay attention to what Price calls "placement problems" (NWR 5–6). If we claim that all reality is ultimately natural reality, then "how are we to 'place' moral facts, mathematical facts, meaning facts, and so on? How are we to locate topics of these kinds within a naturalistic framework, thus conceived?" (NWR 6). Placement issues are precisely the issues that naturalists and their opponents fight over:

> In cases of this kind, we seemed to be faced with a choice between forcing the topic concerned into a category which for one reason or another seems ill-shaped to contain it, or regarding it as at best second-rate—not a genuine area of fact or knowledge. (Ibid.)

This dilemma is reminiscent of one of the pressures on naturalism that Stroud identifies. If we have a very restrictive sense of what constitutes natural objects (for example, only physical objects), then there is a pressure to distort or even deny the very phenomena that naturalism is supposed to explain. "Thus," Price writes, "placement problems provide the motivation for much contemporary opposition to naturalism in philosophy" (NWR 6–7). To the critics of naturalism, the "solutions" to placement problems that naturalists propose are completely unsatisfactory; they distort the very phenomena that they seek to explain. But, as Price argues, we are not limited to the choice between some version of object naturalism and non-naturalism. There is a *third* alternative—an alternative that is very close to Dewey's naturalism. We can be naturalistic in a different key by "[rejecting] *object* naturalism, in favor of a subject-naturalist approach to the same theoretical problems" (NWR 7). Subject naturalism—like Dewey's naturalism—rests on the fact that we humans are natural creatures. Dewey's emphasis on the continuity between experience and nature is his way of emphasizing the priority of subject naturalism. Price, taking account of post-Fregean forms of semantic representationalism, is ruthlessly critical of all forms of representationalism. That is why he characterizes his naturalism as a "naturalism without representationalism."[107] By paying attention to the linguistic turn in philosophy, Price supports his thesis about the priority of subject naturalism with nuance and analytic sophistication. But the upshot of his naturalism without representationalism is substantively close to Dewey's naturalism.

There is another respect in which Price's subject naturalism supports Dewey's naturalism. For Dewey, there is a *plurality* of types of human inquiry.[108] For Price, there is a plurality of

> *ways of talking*, of forms of human linguistic behaviour. The challenge is now simply to explain in naturalistic terms how creatures like us come to talk in these various ways. This is a matter of explaining what role the different language games play in our lives—what differences there are between the functions of talk of value and the functions of talk of electrons, for example. (NWR 20)

Dewey, who was unaware of the later work of Wittgenstein, does not speak of "language games." But Price's point is compatible with the way in which Dewey speaks of a plurality of types of inquiry. Even Price's talk about a plurality of *functions* is reminiscent of Dewey. I do not want to underestimate the differences between Price and Dewey—differences that result from Price's taking account of the problematic features of post-Fregean semantic forms of representationalism and his emphasis on the plurality of ways of

talking—a plurality of language games. However, I want to emphasize the manner in which Price's subject naturalism fits within a
tradition of pluralistic pragmatic naturalism articulated by Dewey.

I have been discussing a number of contemporary philosophers who have been influenced by Dewey in developing their
versions of pragmatic naturalism—Rorty, Brandom, Putnam,
Godfrey-Smith, Kitcher, and Price. But I have also been arguing
that, quite independent of any direct influence by Dewey, there is
a movement away from "restricted," "reductive," and "bald naturalism." There is also a movement away from the type of
Kantianism that insists that there is an unbridgeable gap between
conceptual normativity and nature. We are moving closer to a
Deweyan naturalism where there is continuity with difference—a
Deweyan, pluralistic pragmatic naturalism informed by the analytical sophistication of the linguistic turn.

In *Articulating the World*, Rouse does not mention Dewey, but
his version of philosophical naturalism reads like Dewey brought
up to date. I will limit myself to some of the highlights of this
densely argued book that seeks to take account of the numerous
recent debates related to naturalism. Rouse approaches the topic
of philosophical naturalism in a distinctive manner. Taking philosophical naturalism as an ongoing historical project, he argues that
defenders of this project must be prepared to meet the new challenges of their critics:

> The book is motivated by a specific conception of the
> current situation in the philosophical understanding of
> naturalism. The most pressing challenge for naturalism
> today is to show how to account for our own capacities
> for scientific understanding as a natural phenomenon that
> could be understood scientifically. Naturalist views that
> cannot meet this challenge would be self-defeating. The
> principal claim of the book is that meeting this challenge
> requires substantial, complementary revisions to familiar
> philosophical accounts of both of its components: how
> to situate our conceptual capacities within a scientific un-
> derstanding of the world and what a scientific conception
> of the world amounts to. (AW 6–7)

More specifically, his purpose is to show that we can give a naturalistic, philosophical, and scientific account of the normative conceptual abilities that have been the primary concern of Sellars, McDowell, Brandom, and John Haugeland (AW 10–2). Rouse seeks to "advance a broadly Sellarsian philosophical naturalism by rethinking *both* the manifest and scientific images" in order to show how they can be reconciled (AW 13; emphasis added). He refers to the famous (some might say infamous) distinction between the manifest and the scientific images of man-in-the-world (AW 7–8) that Sellars outlined in his essay "Philosophy and the Scientific Image of Man." Because many thinkers pick up on Sellars's language of the manifest and the scientific images, we need to clarify how Sellars originally used these expressions.

Sellars begins his essay with his provocative description of the aim of philosophy: "The aim of philosophy, abstractly formulated, is to understand how things in the broadest possible sense of the term hang together in the broadest possible sense of the term" (PSI 1). In order to achieve this aim, philosophy must develop a synoptic vision that fuses two different competing images of man-in-the-world (PSI 4).[109] The manifest image is the one in which man first encounters himself as man (PSI 6). The primary objects in the manifest image are *persons* (PSI 9)—and (among other things) persons are creatures capable of having concepts, making judgments, and performing inferences—in short, engaging in the intentional activity of reasoning. The manifest image can also be characterized as a scientific image in a limited sense— it is limited to "correlational induction" (PSI 7). In contrast to the manifest image, Sellars stipulates that the scientific image employs the postulational techniques required for *explanatory* scientific theories. Consequently, it can also be called the "postulational . . . image" (ibid.). The primary objects of the scientific image turn out to be "complex physical [systems]" (PSI 25). We achieve knowledge of these physical objects by employing postulational techniques for scientific explanation (PSI 19–20).[110] Each of these images claims to be "*the* true and, in principle, *complete* account of man-in-the-world" (PSI 25). But these competing images clash with each other. So the problem for philosophy is how to resolve this clash of two images. How are we to evaluate the claims of these two images to be the true and complete account of man-in-the-world?[111] Ever since the rise of modern science, philosophers have struggled with the competing claims of these two images. Sellars argues that most of the "solutions" offered by modern philosophers—from Descartes to the present—turn out to be problematic (PSI 26–31). Sellars affirms that ultimately the scientific image has ontological and epistemological *primacy* (PSI 32). This is the point of his categorical statement, namely, that he is prepared to say that (*speaking as a philosopher*) in the dimension of describing and explaining the world, science and science alone "is the measure of all things, of what is that it is, and of what is not that it is not" (EPM 83).

One of Sellars's favored examples to illustrate what he means is the relation of the Boyle-Charles law to the kinetic theory of molecules (see, for example, EPM 48). The Boyle-Charles law tells us that at a fixed temperature the volume of a gas is inversely proportional to the pressure exerted by the gas. This is an empirical law based on observations that are performed in the manifest image; it does not involve any unobservable postulated entities. But a kinetic theory that postulates unobservable microphysical objects can scientifically explain such an empirical law. In such cases, microphysical theories thus

> *explain empirical laws by explaining why observable things obey to the extent that they do, these empirical laws;* that is, they explain why individual objects of various kinds and in various circumstances in the observation framework behave in those ways in which it has been inductively established that they do behave. Roughly, it is because a gas is—in some sense of "is"—a cloud of molecules which are behaving in certain theoretically defined ways, that it obeys the *empirical* Boyle-Charles law.[112]

It is microphysical theory (that involves postulated entities) that scientifically explains the empirical Boyle-Charles law. Of course, Sellars affirms the doctrine of fallibility. Consequently, any given scientific theory may be replaced by a better scientific theory. But then, it is the better theory that comes closer to telling us what is—closer in intimating to us "true reality."

But what about the status of persons? Can talk about persons be reconstructed in the language of the scientific image? Sellars not only denies that such a reconstruction is possible, he makes a much stronger claim: "For it can, I believe, be conclusively shown that such a reconstruction is in principle impossible, the impossibility in question being a strictly logical one" (PSI 38). We seem to be left with the awkward conclusion that although the scientific image has ontological and epistemological primacy, it cannot account for persons—the primary objects of the manifest image. And that, as Sellars himself says, "would seem to be the end of the matter" (ibid.). But like a cliffhanger, we have not yet reached the end of the story—the final denouement. In what might seem like an all-too-rapid finale, Sellars tells us that the framework of persons (which can almost be defined as beings with intentions) can be joined with the scientific image. Here is his grand finale:

> Thus the conceptual framework of persons is not something that needs to be *reconciled with* the scientific image, but rather something to be *joined* to it. Thus, to complete the scientific image we need to enrich it *not* with more ways of saying what is the case, but with the language of community and individual intentions, so that by construing the actions we intend to do and the circumstances in which we intend to do them in scientific terms, we *directly* relate to the world as conceived by scientific theory to our purposes, and make it *our* world and no longer an alien appendage to the world in which we do our living. We can, of course, as matters now stand, realize this direct incorporation of the scientific image into our way of life only in imagination. But to do so is, if only in imagination, to transcend the dualism of the manifest and scientific images of man-in-the-world. (PSI 40)

Most followers of Sellars—even his most fervid admirers—have not been happy with this all-too-quick "joining" of the scientific and the manifest images.[113] Nevertheless, we can give a sympathetic account of what Sellars intends. He wants—to use a Hegelian turn of phrase—to bring out the "truth" that is implicit in both the scientific and the manifest images of man-in-the-world in order to achieve a unified, synoptic, and *stereoscopic* vision of man-in-the-world (PSI 19). I stress "stereoscopic" because we need to keep our eyes focused on the "truth" implicit in both images. If we focus exclusively on the scientific image, then we will end up with an account that leaves out what is most essential about human beings— their personhood. And if we focus exclusively on the objects of the manifest image—persons who have intentions—, we will end up with a distorted picture of science. Science will turn out to be derivative or secondary. Science (falsely) will turn out to be not only methodologically but substantively dependent on the manifest image.

Just as many thinkers inspired by Hegel fell into two camps of left and right Hegelians, so an analogous phenomenon has occurred with those inspired by Sellars. Left Sellarsians find that what Sellars has to say from a manifest point of view about concepts, belief, thinking, knowledge, meaning, rules, language, intentionality (and related concepts) is much more productive and fruitful than what he has to say about science and the scientific image. Philosophers such as Brandom, McDowell, and Haugeland challenge the Sellarsian claim about the epistemological and ontological priority of the scientific image. They make an even stronger claim. Rouse states their view succinctly:

> A radically comprehensive naturalism would undermine its own intelligibility as a conception of the world. The scientific image and the understanding that it promises depend upon our capacities for conceptual understanding and its rational accountability. These very capacities for conceptual thought cannot be fully assimilated within the terms of a scientific understanding of nature. (AW 11)

We see here the specter of the type of Kantianism that insists that a scientific understanding of nature *presupposes* a philosophical understanding of our rational capacities.

Right Sellarsians (for example, Paul Churchland, Millikan, and Dennett, among others) are much more impressed by Sellars's scientific realism and his claims about the explanatory power of science—so much so that they think that there is nothing about the manifest image that cannot, in principle, be reconstructed or replaced by the scientific image. Right Sellarsians are the successors of those who have always held that science and science alone is the source and standard for achieving knowledge of the world. Left Sellarsians are the successors of Kant who claims that neither theoretical nor practical rationality can be adequately explained by the natural sciences.

Sellars himself was neither a left nor a right Sellarsian, just as Hegel was neither a right nor a left Hegelian. It is almost as if their successors cannot quite hold together in a single vision what Sellars (and Hegel) claimed *must* be held together. In Sellars's terminology, a unified philosophic vision of man-in-the-world must be stereoscopic. In addition to the now entrenched distinction between right and left Sellarsians, we need a third category—centrist Sellarsians. These are the interpreters and followers of Sellars who try to keep true to the spirit, if not the letter, of his stereoscopic vision and show how we can form a single unified vision that does justice to both the scientific and the manifest images.[114]

Rouse, in developing his version of a philosophical naturalism, follows Sellars in his attempt to do justice to the insights of the manifest and the scientific images. But to do this he introduces significant revisions of both these images—revisions that take account of the debates that have occurred since the publication of "Philosophy and the Scientific Image." In defending his version of philosophical naturalism, Rouse's strategy departs from many other naturalists who think that left Sellarsians make too much fuss about the *sui generis* character of conceptual normativity. On the contrary, he thinks that Brandom, McDowell, and Haugeland "advance the naturalist cause constructively. . . . [since] by showing where currently influential versions of naturalism fall short, they highlight the requirements for a more adequate naturalistic self-understanding" (AW 12). Although Rouse disagrees with these thinkers on many technical details, he basically agrees with their insistence on the distinctive normativity of our conceptual capacities.[115] He emphatically disagrees with them insofar as they claim that this puts our conceptual capacities "beyond" natural scientific understanding and explanation.[116] Their critique of naturalism is based upon familiar but inadequate conceptions of science. Once we develop a more adequate, open-ended, practice-oriented conception of science, then there are no *a priori* reasons for claiming that we cannot give a scientific account of conceptual normativity.[117]

Dewey would entirely agree with Rouse's assertion that "naturalism in philosophy is only viable if scientific understanding is a natural phenomenon that intelligibly belongs within a scientific conception of the world" (AW 201). Naturalists recognize not only the fallibility of current science but also "the fallibility of prevailing conceptions of science" (AW 202). Rouse, like many pragmatists, is critical of a representationalist conception of scientific understanding. His practice-oriented understanding of science stresses that science is a future-oriented research enterprise where the sciences continually revise the terms and inferential relations through which we understand the world (see AW 246).[118] As Rouse develops his practice-oriented conception of scientific activity, he sounds more and more like Dewey. Rouse argues

> that conceptual understanding in the sciences involves material, social, and discursive transformations of the human environment taken together. These transformations amount to extensive forms of niche construction . . . . An environmental niche is not something specifiable apart from the way of life of an organism, which in turn cannot be understood except in its specific patterns of interdependence with its environment. A niche is thus a configuration of the world itself as relevant to an ongoing pattern of activity. (AW 215)

It should be clear by now that Rouse takes up the obligation for critical reflection where McDowell urges philosophical restraint. In opposition to McDowell (and others), who reject a naturalistic approach to our conceptual abilities, Rouse's aim of advancing "a broadly Sellarsian philosophical naturalism" (AW 13) has, I think, much in common with Dewey's naturalism.[119] It is this affinity that I want to consider by highlighting certain aspects of Rouse's richly argued work. When Rouse claims that recent "philosophical and empirical studies of the sciences thereby encourage reconceiving the scientific image as incorporating a situated practical capacity to extend and refine current understanding of ourselves-in-the-world rather than consisting in a systematic representation" (AW 15), he echoes Dewey's emphasis on scientific inquiry as a future-oriented and self-reflective set of practices. There is also an affinity with Kitcher's characterization of Dewey's naturalism as methodological (rather than substantive). Rouse shows how recent developments in biological theory, evolutionary theory, ecology, and niche theory help to support a naturalistic account of humans-in-the-world:

> The emergence of the mid-twentieth-century evolutionary synthesis provided powerful new conceptual resources for philosophical naturalists. Evolutionary theory offered promising possibilities for understanding the normativity of knowledge and conceptual content in terms of genetic processes that secure biological adaptation to an organism's environment. . . . New theoretical developments within evolutionary theory (e.g., developmental evolution, developmental systems theory, ecological-developmental biology, and niche construction theory), along with new empirical work on animal behavior, human evolution, and language, now challenge familiar ways of thinking about cognition and knowledge in evolutionary terms and suggest alternative approaches for situating human understanding within our evolutionary trajectory. Philosophical naturalism commits us to maintaining an ongoing engagement with scientific work in this way without settling for familiar and congenial conceptual horizons that the sciences continue to surpass. (AW 16)

These are extremely ambitious claims. What is impressive about Rouse's book is the extent to which he supports these general claims with detailed arguments. In this respect, there is a similarity with the way in which Godfrey-Smith supports his version of naturalism by an appeal to recent developments in evolutionary theory. They both approach the question of naturalism in the way in which Dewey advocated—where one takes account of the best scientific *practices* of one's time.

To illustrate how close Rouse is to Dewey, consider what he has to say about the organism-environment connection of biological creatures: An organism's biological environment does not consist of its physical surrounding but rather consists of the surrounding environment that matters to its development (AW 100–2). Rouse thus appeals to recent developments in niche theory:

> Niche construction is the transformation of the developmental, selective environment of an organism and its lineage by ongoing, cumulative interactions of other organisms with that environment. The biological environment of an organism's lineage thus is not simply given but is instead *dynamically shaped by ongoing interaction* with the organisms in that lineage. (AW 20; emphasis added)

This is the very language that Dewey used in his critique of the mechanical reflex arc concept. The Deweyan character of Rouse's naturalism becomes even clearer when he affirms that "conceptual understanding thus emerges biologically as a highly flexible, self-reproducing and self-differentiating responsiveness to cumulatively constructed aspects of our selective environment" (AW 21). This is a naturalism of continuity with difference, not a reductive naturalism and not an epistemological theory of the non-natural "purity" of conceptual abilities.

I have been telling a story that leads us through what seem like the chaotic debates about naturalism—one with many twists and turns but an overarching coherence. After my introductory remarks about the pitfalls and opposing pressures that one confronts, I recalled the vigorous discussion of naturalism that took place in America during the early decades of the twentieth century. With the growing dominance of the analytic style of philosophizing and the so-called "linguistic turn," this tradition of American naturalism was almost totally obliterated. The "new" discourse about naturalism initiated by Quine and Sellars in the mid-twentieth century barely made any reference to this earlier tradition.[120] I then presented a brief sketch of Dewey's naturalism and his affirmation of the continuity of experience and nature. Most professional philosophers trained in the analytic style of philosophy ignored Dewey or viewed him in a patronizing manner—as a thinker who had good intentions but nevertheless lacked analytic finesse in philosophical argumentation. Even a sympathetic interpreter of Dewey's pragmatism and naturalism like Brandom challenged Dewey's continuity thesis, claiming that the latter—and more generally, the classical American pragmatists—failed to present a clear demarcation and explication of the conceptual abilities that are distinctive of sapient creatures.

In the mid-twentieth century the relevance of Kant was rediscovered—especially the Kant who clearly set forth the distinction between what McDowell calls a "disenchanted" concept of nature that lacked any meaning and normativity, and reason—*Verstand* and *Vernunft*—which is the source of both theoretical and practical normativity. The key figure for many American philosophers in this rehabilitation of Kant was Sellars (although one should not underestimate the importance of Peter Strawson on the other side of the Atlantic). This Kantian turn presented a serious challenge to standard forms of naturalism. McDowell sought to appropriate Kant—especially the Kant who emphasizes the *sui generis* character of spontaneity—and to combine this with a new/old Aristotelian understanding of human nature as second nature. McDowell claimed that once we appreciate the significance of second nature (as opposed to first nature), we can advocate a liberal naturalism— a naturalism that combines the insights of Kant and Aristotle. For McDowell, the task of philosophical inquiry is to uncover and expose the faulty assumptions and presuppositions that are the source of philosophical anxieties. Once this task is performed, there is no further philosophical work to be done. For McDowell, we do not have to engage in "constructive philosophizing."

We have seen that philosophers such as Godfrey-Smith, Kitcher, and Rouse seriously question this quietism. They agree with McDowell that we have to revise our conception of nature but maintain that simply proposing a concept of second nature is not enough. In a Deweyan spirit, they argue that there is important philosophical work to be done in showing how new developments in sciences—especially those sciences that deal with the biological, evolutionary, and cultural dimensions of human life—are crucial for developing an adequate philosophical naturalism. They react (as Dewey did) to what they take to be the obsession with epistemological issues that is divorced from looking at and seeing what we can learn from new developments in the sciences.

More generally, there has been a philosophical movement away from the various forms of "bald," "reductive," or "restricted naturalism"—the types of naturalism that Stroud described as distorting the very phenomena that a naturalistic study is supposed to explain. We are also moving away from a type of Kantianism that insists on an unbridgeable dichotomy between nature and reason. We are moving closer to an understanding of humans-in-the-world where there is a Deweyan continuity with difference. In Price's terms, this is a form of subject naturalism—a naturalism that has priority over object naturalism. No one wants to deny that something extraordinary happened in the course of evolution—the emergence of the full capacity to engage in discourse that requires linguistic mastery, the capacity to draw inferences, and the ability to give and ask for reasons. But once we open ourselves to a more pragmatic open-ended conception of scientific inquiry, and are responsive to what we continue to learn from sciences that pertain to our biological and social nature, we have good reason to endorse a *pragmatic naturalism*—a naturalism that seeks to understand the ways in which we as human beings are continuous not only with other animate creatures but also with the rest of nature. We are coming closer to Dewey's vision of continuity with difference and his call for a reconstruction of philosophy—a reconstruction that breaks away from an excessive concern with the sharpening of analytic tools. There is an opportunity to use these refined analytic techniques to deal with the significant problems of human beings. This is the type of reconstruction that Dewey called for in his time, and that Kitcher and others seek to develop for our time.

Let me place this movement to a more liberal pragmatic naturalism in a larger philosophical context. Many philosophical debates today are haunted by the specters of Kant and Hegel, including the debates about naturalism. Sometimes this is epitomized in the phrase "naturalism and normativity," or more sharply "naturalism *versus* normativity." Some (but not all) Kantians insist that there is a sharp and categorical distinction between a "disenchanted" nature that is the subject matter of the natural science and the normativity that is characteristic of theoretical and practical reason. This categorical distinction seems to be well supported by a conception of normativity as involving what we should or *ought* to do when contrasted with a conception of the natural world where we speak about what *is* (or what are the facts). In many everyday contexts, we do—and indeed *must*—make this distinction between *what is* and *what ought to be*. But what is the philosophical significance of this distinction?

Kantians (or, more cautiously, some Kantians) think that this is the reason why we must draw a sharp distinction between nature and freedom, as well as between nature and reason. Reason is the source of normativity that is lacking in nature. I have already shown how somebody like McDowell, in considering the various dualisms that modern philosophy seeks to bridge, holds that this approach is reflective of a "deeper dualism" of norm and nature (MW 93). "What is debatable," McDowell contends, "is how we ought to respond to the deeper dualism" (MW 94). In a quasi-Hegelian move, he asserts that there is no gulf to be bridged, no gap that has to be closed. He thinks that his ideas of second nature and *Bildung* are sufficient to reveal the illusion of a gap between nature and norm. It is as if McDowell makes a move from Kantian naturalism to Hegelian naturalism.

Hegelians, including Hegelian pragmatists who sometimes appeal to Aristotle, are critical of blowing up the distinction between nature and normativity into a philosophical dichotomy. Hegel takes up the Kantian dichotomies—nature and freedom, phenomena and noumena, spontaneity and receptivity, sensibility and understanding—in order to show that these dichotomies are unstable and that, when properly understood, they turn out to be moments in *dynamic* organic unity in which there is identity with difference. After Darwin and with contemporary developments in sciences such as biology, neuroscience, cognitive science, and ecology, there have been attempts to naturalize Kant and naturalize Hegel. Dewey and the early American pragmatic naturalists were clearly on the side of Hegel. They thought that Darwinian evolutionary theory supported the thesis of continuity with difference.

With the pioneering work of Sellars, the Kantian moment reasserted itself with renewed vigor, although there is clear evidence that Sellars was moving to a more Hegelian naturalism.

My primary thesis is that the recent work by Godfrey-Smith, Kitcher, Price, Rouse, and many others is moving us closer to the spirit of Deweyan philosophical naturalism that overcomes the dualisms that have plagued so much of traditional philosophy, including the dualism of nature and norm. This is a pragmatic naturalism that is open to learning from new forms of scientific inquiry.[121] Of course, there will always be disagreements among philosophers. There are those who think that some version of reductive naturalism or pure physicalism will win out in the end, just as there are philosophers who think that they can demonstrate that all forms of naturalism are ultimately incoherent. And of course, there are still many ongoing and significant disputes among those who think of themselves as liberal pragmatic naturalists. We can acknowledge this diversity and yet clearly affirm that the legacy of Dewey's open-ended and pluralistic naturalism is very much alive today.

4 APPENDIX: SELLARS'S AND DEWEY'S NATURALISM

A full examination of Sellars's naturalism and its relation to Dewey's naturalism would require an independent study. At first glance, they seem to be poles apart. Dewey, especially in *Experience and Nature*, spends a great deal of time and space debunking the philosophical use of "real" that seeks to deny the reality of our commonsense framework of physical objects and what Sellars calls "the manifest image of man-in-the-world." Dewey would reject the claim that the commonsense world of molar physical objects is "unreal."[122] Dewey would also reject Sellars's claim that although the manifest image has *methodological* priority, it is the scientific image that has *substantive* or ontological primacy. When viewed through Price's distinction between object naturalism and subject naturalism, Sellars seems to advocate a type of object naturalism, insofar as he focuses his attention on the primary objects of the manifest and scientific images, whereas Dewey advocates a subject naturalism in which philosophy's starting-point must lie in science's disclosure *about ourselves* (NWR 5). Dewey emphasizes the continuity between nonhuman animals and human beings; Sellars tells us that the move from the pre-conceptual to the conceptual manner of thinking was a "holistic" and unique "jump of awareness" that enabled humans to *become* human (PSI 6). Dewey would question Sellars's assertion that there is a *global* clash of the two images in which each claims to be the true, and in principle, complete account of man-in-the-world. This is not to deny that throughout the history of modern science there have been significant and dramatic *local* clashes between what we learn from the sciences and some of our commonsense beliefs. We give up some beliefs because of what we learn from scientific inquiry. We (unless we are pathological) no longer believe that the earth is flat, that there is spontaneous generation, or that there are "real" demons. Furthermore, we know that scientists can tell us a great deal about the atomic and subatomic structures of the molar physical objects that we encounter in everyday life, but this is not a reason to doubt that we encounter such objects in our daily lives and take them to be real. In Dewey's naturalism there is nothing quite like "picturing," which Sellars takes to be essential for a naturalistic theory of linguistic and cognitive representation. Dewey would reject the need for any such picturing relation.

But although first appearances are important, we need to be wary of them. Sellars is a very complex thinker, and there are several strands in his thinking that reveal a closer affinity with Dewey's pragmatic naturalism. To show this, I want to begin with some historical considerations. Sellars's father, Roy Wood Sellars, was one of the leading members of the American naturalist movement that dominated the early decades of the twentieth century. Although Roy Wood had his disagreements with Dewey, they shared a great deal in common. Both were strong advocates of evolutionary naturalism. The following striking passage from Roy Wood's *Evolutionary Naturalism* might have appeared in Dewey's *Experience and Nature*:

> Knowing is surely a natural operation resting upon evolved abilities. To give a naturalistic explanation of it is . . . to give a crowning touch to science itself. Nature is a world in which knowing occurs, just as surely as it is a world in which coal burns and dynamite explodes.[123]

Dewey and Roy Wood Sellars also shared a commitment to humanism and signed the 1933 Humanist Manifesto.[124]

Wilfrid frequently affirmed his affinity with his father's philosophical outlook. Fabio Gironi has written an excellent study of the philosophical relationship between Wilfrid and Roy Wood Sellars, using both published and unpublished documents.[125] He shows Wilfrid's deep indebtedness to his father's philosophy and brings out some of their differences that are the results of Wilfrid's "Kantian, normatively-saturated naturalism."[126] In a paper presented at a symposium in his father's honor in 1954, Wilfrid wrote that

> a discerning student of philosophy, familiar with the writings of Sellars *pere*, who chances to read Sellars *fils*, and is

not taken in by the superficial changes of idiom and emphasis which reflect the adaptation of the species to a new
environment, will soon be struck by the fundamental
identity of outlook. The identity is obscured by differences of terminology, method and polemical orientation,
but it is none the less an identity. How natural, then, and,
in a sense how true to say that Critical Realism, Evolutionary Naturalism, and all that they imply, are part of my
parental inheritance.[127]

Unlike many of his contemporary analytic philosophers, Wilfrid Sellars had a deep philosophical connection with early
American naturalism. There are several other dimensions of
Sellars's philosophy that also bring him closer to Dewey. Recall
that when Sellars suggests that the manifest image may be false
and that, *speaking as a philosopher*, he is prepared to deny the reality
of the commonsense world of physical objects, he clarifies his remark by saying, "Or, to put it less paradoxically, that in the
dimension of *describing* and explaining the world, science is the
measure of all things, of what is that it is, and of what is not that
it is not" (EPM 83; emphasis added). Now it is clear that Sellars in
this context is using "describing" and "explaining" in a very technical sense—one that needs to be explained and justified, because
it is obvious that there are many uses of "describing" and "explaining" (as Wittgenstein has taught us) that are perfectly appropriate
to the manifest image. We could not engage in correlational induction unless we describe what we observe. There are many ways in
which we use "explain" in the manifest image. When asked why
we are doing something, we explain our actions by indicating what
we intend to achieve. Even if we accept Sellars's depiction of the
manifest image, we clearly describe and explain all sorts of things
and events within this image. Sellars certainly knows this. So we
need to ask: What is the *technical* sense of "description" and "explanation" that is exclusively appropriate to the scientific image?

It turns out that this is not such an easy question to answer.[128]
Willem deVries, who has written extensively about Sellars and
knows his work thoroughly, confesses that he has "increasingly
come to doubt that we can make sense of the ideal of a 'pure

descriptive core to language.' For one thing, I doubt that such a notion is, in fact, a part or requirement of naturalism."[129] DeVries claims that the appeal to pure description "is a version of what Price calls and castigates as 'object naturalism.'"[130] Furthermore, deVries notes that, paradoxically, it is Sellars himself who undermines the ideal of a pure descriptive core to language:

> But there is no reason, given Sellars's holistic and functionalistic treatment of the semantic, to believe that (1) there is or could be any isolable purely descriptive domain in language, or (2) such a purified descriptive language could *replace* the languages we currently know and love. The fact that it is a bedrock function of language to prepare and orchestrate action should make us suspicious of the notion of pure description.[131]

In effect, deVries argues (as Dewey might argue) that there is something suspicious about the Sellarsian claim that "one would expect there to be a sense in which the scientific picture of the world *replaces* the commonsense picture; a sense in which the scientific account of 'what there is' *supersedes* the descriptive ontology of everyday life" (EPM 82).

The sting of Sellars's remark about description and explanation in the scientific image is blunted when we realize that he comes very close to saying something like the following: There is a distinctive sense of "description" and "explanation" that is appropriate to the scientific image of man-in-the-world. When we endorse *this distinctive sense*, then it follows that science is the measure of what is and what is not. But this is perfectly compatible with saying that there are other senses (uses) of "description" and "explanation" that are characteristic of the manifest image, and that it makes good sense to say that the molar physical objects of our commonsense framework are real. Indeed, Sellars himself defends a form of "direct realism" when we are functioning in the manifest image. Translating this into Dewey's language, we might say that there is a perfectly good sense of "real" in which we can speak of commonsense molar objects as real, and a perfectly good sense of "real" where we can speak of scientific objects as real. And these different claims are compatible, although sometimes they clash, and consequently we need to make adjustments. Sellars, in his peculiar twist of Kant, wants to maintain that "the perceptual world is phenomenal in something like the Kantian sense."[132] However, "the real or 'noumenal' world which supports 'the world of appearances' is not a *metaphysical* world of unknowable things in themselves, but simply the world as construed by scientific theory."[133] But for Kant the world of appearances is empirically real.[134] In short, if we take a more relaxed and open pragmatic stance, we can say that there are different but not incompatible ways of speaking about what is "real" that apply to both the manifest image and the scientific image. DeVries concludes his study of the clash between the manifest image and the scientific image by declaring that "the right way to think of the relation between the manifest image and the scientific image is as a matter of *mutual accommodation*, not one-way dominance."[135] Dewey would emphatically agree.

There are still other aspects of Sellars's philosophical reflections that bring him closer to pragmatic naturalism. What do humans turn out to be for Sellars? "The scientific image of man turns out to be that of a complex physical system" (PSI 25). No naturalist will deny that we can study and learn a great deal about human beings as complex physical systems—certainly not Dewey. The interesting and controversial issues arise for naturalists when we claim that human beings are "more" than mere physical systems. And of course, Sellars, with his stereoscopic vision, clearly thinks that human beings are "more" than complex physical systems—they are persons. This does not mean that we have to countenance any extra-special substances or entities to account for persons, in the manner of Descartes. It turns out that the complex physical system that we call a human being can *do* all sorts of interesting things and *perform* all sorts of interesting *functions*. These physical systems can speak, think, form individual and community intentions, give and ask for reasons, draw inferences, and willfully act. In short, the complex physical systems that we identify as human beings can do all the things that the category of persons in the manifest image do. Although we can study human beings insofar as they are complex physical systems, we also want some account of how humans become creatures who are able to follow conceptual norms and obey rules. We want some account of how human minds are *embodied*. Once again, deVries is helpful. In "Language, Norms, and Linguistic Norms," he argues that

> Sellars did not, but *should* have recognized a form of natural normativity that derives from the functionality of biological processes and structures. This form of natural normativity is not reductive, but it *is* naturalistic. It is also a precondition of intentionality, and recognizing how it conditions intentionality helps to disarm the all-too-common notion that intentionality forces either dualism or even idealism upon us.[136]

DeVries' aim is not so much to criticize Sellars but to show how his naturalism can be enriched. Drawing on Hegel, deVries argues that Sellars ought to have paid more attention to a form of natural normativity that is exhibited by the goal-directness of the structure and function of organisms.[137] He asserts that recognizing natural normativity as a mediating link to conceptual normativity can strengthen Sellars's stance:

> It does better justice to the structure of our thinking about biological matters, for one thing. But it also helps fill in the gap between supposedly full-fledged normativity of rule-obeying consciousnesses and the merely mechanical world in which they operate and from which they somehow emerge. It seems utterly unintelligible how a collection of material objects could be or become a rule-obeying person, *without some further mediating structures*.[138]

This is precisely the point that Dewey would make. Dewey's continuity thesis is intended to show that there are mediating structures that enable us to understand how our "higher" cognitive abilities (including "full-fledged normativity of rule-obeying consciousness"), which are shaped by our social and cultural interactions, are nevertheless grounded in our biological organic nature.

Ironically, it is Sellars who has worked out in detail a pragmatic, intersubjective (social) understanding of language and thought. We need to recognize that there are autonomous discourses, such as semantic discourse and modal discourse, that are not reducible to descriptive discourse. It makes eminently good sense that philosophers such as Rorty and Brandom think of Sellars as a key figure in the pragmatic tradition who emphasizes our *know-how*. Stressing this way of reading Sellars—where human beings are capable of engaging in a plurality of different types of discourse or language games—brings him very close to Price's Deweyan subject naturalism, despite Sellars's focus on the primary *objects* of the scientific and manifest image. Price's statement about the plurality of our ways of talking, and the role that the various and complex language games play in our lives (NWR 20), is just as applicable to Sellars.

In the conclusion of his book on Sellars, deVries returns to a reconsideration of Sellars's synoptic, stereoscopic vision, which shows just how close Sellars is to Dewey's pragmatic naturalism. DeVries reminds us that "it is persons who inhabit the logical space of reasons and can use or apply the methods and canons of science to produce a picture of reality. *Science is something people do*."[139] He then comments:

> I do not see any coherent way for Sellars to deny the reality of persons, but there is reality and there is reality. Persons are *practically real*, and they are practically real because they make themselves such. Practical reality is a matter of the truth of prescriptive and normative claims, and that, in turn, is a matter of recognized, intersubjectively held, intersubjectively applicable, shared intentions. The existentialist turns of phrase Sellars uses at the beginning of "Philosophy and the Scientific Image of Man" to describe the emergence of human (self-)consciousness are not a fluke or joke on his part. Humanity's self-recognition as humanity is the *fons et origo* of humanity. It is in this context that Sellars's reflexivity requirement falls into place as absolutely central to his entire philosophy.[140]

Sellars does not use the expression "practical reality," but deVries is describing something that is "absolutely central" for Sellars. If we think of "practical reality" as designating what is distinctive about persons, and "empirical reality" as the object of scientific inquiry, then we see how practical reality and empirical reality are not only compatible but are mutually bound to each other. Sellars believes that we should continually adjust our practical reality to what we learn about empirical reality from scientific inquiry. So does Dewey. But Sellars is also telling us that we can never abandon our practical reality. And this has always been Dewey's fundamental claim. In short, Sellars's synoptic, stereoscopic vision is one that affirms the practical reality of persons *and* the empirical reality that we are in the process of discovering through science.

Finally, I want to turn to how Sellars understands normativity. The subtitle of James O'Shea's study of Sellars is revealing: "Naturalism with a Normative Turn." Although the expression "normative" is not one of Dewey's favored expressions, his naturalism, which cuts across the fact/value dichotomy, might also be called a "naturalism with a normative turn." Both thinkers take human beings to be thoroughly natural creatures who are capable of engaging in moral, social, and political discourses and actions. Neither philosopher thinks that we have to introduce any supernatural entities or faculties to give an account of humans-in-the-world. Sellars can be read as providing an account of normativity that includes conceptual normativity characteristic of thinking, reasoning, knowing, and communicating. This is compatible with a robust naturalism. Despite Sellars's appropriation of Kantian themes and Dewey's appropriation of Hegelian themes, neither philosopher subscribes to the thesis that there is an unbridgeable dualism—a gap—between naturalism and normativity. Both would affirm that there is no gap to be bridged. Finally, both are committed to an evolutionary naturalism that recognizes that the human species is continuous with the rest of nature. Both affirm that human beings can intentionally act in a manner that enables them to *reconstruct* their world. So, on many fundamental issues, they share a common vision of humans-in-the-world.

NOTES

1. For example, Carl Sachs writes, "This work is animated by a commitment to what I call transcendental naturalism: the view that transcendentally-specified roles must have empirically-specifiable role-players" (Carl B. Sachs, *Intentionality and the Myths of the Given: Between Pragmatism and Phenomenology* [London: Routledge, 2016], p. 9).

2. Barry Stroud, "The Charm of Naturalism," in *Naturalism in Question*, ed. Mario De Caro and David Macarthur (Cambridge: Harvard University Press, 2004), pp. 21–2.

3. Ibid., p. 22.

4. John McDowell, "Naturalism in the Philosophy of Mind," in *Naturalism in Question*, pp. 91–105; see also John McDowell, "Two Sorts of Naturalism," chap. 9 of *Mind, Value, and Reality* (Cambridge: Harvard University Press, 1998), pp. 167–97.

5. John Dewey, *Experience and Nature*, vol. 1 of *The Later Works of John Dewey, 1925–1953*, ed. Jo Ann Boydston (Carbondale: Southern Illinois University Press, 1981); henceforth EN, followed by page number.

6. Hilary Putnam, "Naturalism, Realism, and Normativity," in *Naturalism, Realism, and Normativity*, ed. Mario De Caro (Cambridge: Harvard University Press, 2016), p. 22.

7. Ibid.; Putnam cites Mario De Caro and David Macarthur, "The Nature of Naturalism," introduction to *Naturalism in Question*, pp. 1–17.

8. For a representative sample of the writings of the American naturalists, see John Ryder, ed., *American Philosophic Naturalism in the Twentieth Century* (Amherst, NY: Prometheus Books, 1994).

9. See Joseph Rouse, *Articulating the World: Conceptual Understanding and the Scientific Image* (Chicago: University of Chicago Press, 2015), p. 3; henceforth AW, followed by page number.

10. Rouse cites W.V.O. Quine, "Five Milestones of Empiricism," in *Theories and Things* (Cambridge: Harvard University Press, 1981), p. 67.

11. See W.V.O. Quine, "Things and Their Place in Theories," in *Theories and Things*, pp. 1–23, esp. 21–2; in the same collection of essays, see also "On the Very Idea of a Third Dogma," pp. 38–42, esp. 40; and "Five Milestones of Empiricism," pp. 67–72, esp. 67, 70.

12. See W.V.O. Quine, "Natural Kinds," in *Ontological Relativity and Other Essays* (New York: Columbia University Press, 1969), pp. 114–38, esp. 126–7.

13. See W.V.O. Quine, "Epistemology Naturalized," in *Ontological Relativity and Other Essays*, pp. 69–90.

14. Wilfrid Sellars, *Empiricism and the Philosophy of Mind* (Cambridge: Harvard University Press, 1997), p. 83; henceforth EPM, followed by page number. See the Appendix, where I discuss how this striking claim is open to different interpretations.

15. Immanuel Kant, *Kritik der reiner Vernunft (1787)*, ed. Benno Erdmann, vol. 3 of *Werke*, ed. Wilhelm Dilthey, vols. 1–9 of *Gesammelte Schriften* (Berlin: De Gruyter, 1911), Bxii–xviii; *Critique of Pure Reason*, trans. and ed. Paul Guyer and Allen W. Wood (Cambridge: Cambridge University Press, 1999), Bxii–xviii.

16. Mario De Caro and David Macarthur, "Science, Naturalism, and the Problem of Normativity," introduction to *Naturalism and Normativity*, ed. Mario De Caro and David Macarthur (New York: Columbia University Press, 2010), p. 1. See below my criticism of De Caro and Macarthur's characterization of scientific naturalism.

17. John Dewey, "From Absolutism to Experimentalism," in *The Philosophy of John Dewey: Two Volumes in One*, ed. John J. McDermott (Chicago: University of Chicago Press, 1981), pp. 1–13.

18. Ibid., p. 2.

19. For a detailed historical analysis of how Dewey came to appreciate the significance of evolution and developed his dynamic and dialectical conception of organic-environmental interaction, see Trevor Pearce's forthcoming book, *Pragmatism's Evolution: Organism and Environment in American Philosophy* (Chicago: University of Chicago Press, 2020). Pearce shows how Dewey's integration of Hegel and evolutionary themes shaped his early moral and social philosophy. Pearce's study examines the extensive influence of evolutionary thinking on pragmatic thinkers from 1860 to 1910.

20. Dewey, "From Absolutism to Experimentalism," p. 7.

21. John Dewey to Robert Mark Wenley, December, 1915, in Robert Mark Wenley, *The Life and Work of George Sylvester Morris: A Chapter in the History of American Thought in the Nineteenth Century* (New York: Macmillan, 1917), pp. 316–7. For a superb discussion of the relation of Hegel and Dewey, especially in regard to immanent critique and social life, see Arvi Särkelä, *Immanente Kritik und soziales Leben: Selbsttransformative Praxis nach Hegel und Dewey* (Frankfurt: Klostermann, 2018).

22. John Dewey, "The Present Position of Logical Theory," in *1889–1892: Essays and Outlines of a Critical Theory of Ethics*, vol. 3 of *The Early Works of John Dewey, 1882–1898*, ed. Jo Ann Boydston (Carbondale: Southern Illinois University Press, 1969), p. 134.

23. Ibid., p. 137.

24. Dewey, "From Absolutism to Experimentalism," p. 8.

25. See John Dewey, "The Influence of Darwinism on Philosophy," in *The Philosophy of John Dewey: Two Volumes in One*, pp. 31–41.

26. See John Dewey, "The Reflex Arc Concept in Psychology," in *1895–1898: Early Essays*, vol. 5 of *The Early Works of John Dewey, 1882–1898*, ed. Jo Ann Boydston (Carbondale: Southern Illinois University Press, 1972), pp. 96–109; henceforth RA, followed by page number.

27. See also my discussion of this article in Richard J. Bernstein, "From Hegel to Darwin," chap. 2 of *John Dewey* (Atascadero, CA: Ridgeview Publishing Company, 1966), pp. 15–21.

28. James Mark Baldwin, *Handbook of Psychology: Feeling and Will* (New York: Henry Holt and Company, 1894), p. 60; cited in RA 100.

29. In his 1896 "Philosophy of Education" course, Dewey offers a variation on this theme. He writes, "Adaptation is dynamic, not static. It means control; and highest adaptation means highest control. Environment is not a fixed idea to be measured or set up by kind of life. It is different for every existing creature. There is something to which the organism and the environment are related. The function is something more than organism; it is something more than environment. Organism and environment are simply the two sides of function" (John Dewey, "Lecture III: The Social Value of Education as Reconstructive Control over One's Experience," in pt. 1 of *Education, Logic, Ethics, and Political Philosophy*, vol. 2 of *The Class Lectures of John Dewey, Electronic Edition*, 2nd release, ed. Donald F. Koch and The Center for Dewey Studies [Carbondale: Southern Illinois University, 2015], p. 95, http://www.nlx.com/collections/441 [accessed October 14, 2019]).

30. Trevor Pearce is especially illuminating in showing how Dewey combines Hegel and Darwin in a coherent manner. See his "Hegelianism Needs to Be Darwinism: Evolution and Idealism," in *Pragmatism's Evolution*.

31. Godfrey-Smith points out some of the similarities between Dewey's conception of organic-environment interaction and Richard Lewontin's conception of the dialectical biologist. Dewey would certainly agree with Lewontin's claim that the

environment is a product of the organism, just as the organism is a product of its environment (see Peter Godfrey-Smith, "Organism, Environment, and Dialectics," in *Thinking about Evolution: Historical, Philosophical, and Political Perspectives*, ed. Rama S. Singh, Costas B. Krimbas, Diane B. Paul, and John Beatty [Cambridge: Cambridge University Press, 2001], vol. 2, pp. 253–66).

32. John Dewey, "Experience, Knowledge, and Value: A Rejoinder," in *The Philosophy of John Dewey*, ed. Paul Arthur Schilpp, vol. 1 of *The Library of Living Philosophers*, ed. Paul Arthur Schilpp et al. (New York: Tudor Publishing Company, 1958), p. 544.

33. John Dewey, "The Need for a Recovery of Philosophy," in *1916–1917: Journal Articles, Essays, and Miscellany Published in the 1916–1917 Period*, vol. 10 of *The Middle Works of John Dewey, 1899–1924*, ed. Jo Ann Boydston (Carbondale: Southern Illinois University Press, 1980), pp. 8–9.

34. Robert Brandom, *Perspectives on Pragmatism: Classic, Recent, and Contemporary* (Cambridge: Harvard University Press, 2011), p. 5; henceforth PP, followed by page number.

35. John Dewey, *Logic: The Theory of Inquiry*, vol. 12 of *The Later Works of John Dewey, 1925–1953*, ed. Jo Ann Boydston (Carbondale: Southern Illinois University Press, 1986), pp. 49–50; henceforth LTI, followed by page number.

36. See my discussion of Dewey's conception of quality in Richard J. Bernstein, "Qualitative Immediacy," chap. 7 of *John Dewey*, pp. 89–99.

37. For an excellent account of Dewey's concept of a situation, see Steven Levine, "The Unboundedness of the Situation," in "Pragmatism, Experience, and Answerability," chap. 5 of *Pragmatism, Objectivity, and Experience* (Cambridge: Cambridge University Press, 2019), pp. 182–9.

38. Each of these plateaus incorporates and transforms the natural interactions of the previous plateaus. Thus, the organic incorporates the physical and the plateau of meaning, and

mind incorporates the organic. In his essay "The Inclusive Philosophic Idea," Dewey argues that the social is a distinctive philosophical category that incorporates and transforms the mental, the organic, and the physical. Here, too, the principle of continuity is manifested (see John Dewey, "The Inclusive Philosophic Idea," in *1927–1928: Essays, Reviews, Miscellany, and "Impressions of Soviet Russia,"* vol. 3 of *The Later Works of John Dewey, 1925–1953*, ed. Jo Ann Boydston [Carbondale: Southern Illinois University Press, 1984], pp. 41–54).

39. See also, for example, Richard Rorty, "Comments on Sleeper and Edel," *Transactions of the Charles S. Peirce Society* 21:1 (1985), pp. 39–48, esp. 40.

40. Mark Johnson, *Embodied Mind, Meaning, and Reason: How Our Bodies Give Rise to Understanding* (Chicago: University of Chicago Press, 2017), pp. 40–1. Johnson, inspired by Dewey, develops a theory of embodied mind that takes account of recent developments in cognitive science.

41. Rorty, in one of his early "analytic" papers, makes this pragmatic point: "There is simply no such thing as a method of classifying linguistic expressions that has results guaranteed to remain intact despite the results of future empirical inquiry There is no method which will have the sort of magisterial neutrality of which linguistic philosophers fondly dream" (Richard Rorty, "Mind-Body Identity, Privacy, and Categories," in *Mind, Language, and Metaphilosophy: Early Philosophical Papers*, ed. Stephen Leach and James Tartaglia [Cambridge: Cambridge University Press, 2014], p. 107).

42. Charles Sanders Peirce, *Principles of Philosophy*, ed. Charles Hartshorne and Paul Weiss, vol. 1 of *Collected Papers of Charles Sanders Peirce* (Cambridge: Harvard University Press, 1965), p. 56.

43. See Morris R. Cohen, "Some Difficulties in Dewey's Anthropocentric Naturalism," *Philosophical Review* 49:2 (1940), pp. 196–228.

44. Robert Sinclair, "Anthropocentric Naturalism," in *Pragmatism, Science, and Naturalism*, ed. Jonathan Knowles and Henrik Rydenfelt (Frankfurt: Peter Lang, 2011), pp. 17–8. Sinclair provides an illuminating analysis of Dewey's response to the criticism of his naturalism by his contemporary critics (Santayana and Cohen). He also shows the relevance of Dewey's "anthropocentric naturalism" in his critique of the naturalism of Donald Davidson and McDowell. I think one must be cautious about the expression "anthropocentric naturalism." When Cohen speaks of Dewey's "anthropocentric naturalism," he is using "anthropocentric" in the pejorative sense—to suggest that Dewey is projecting subjective human features onto the rest of nature. Sinclair uses the term in a more neutral sense emphasizing that philosophy should begin with what science tells us about human beings. He characterizes the objections of Cohen and Santayana as the "narcissistic objection"—the objection that "Dewey's use of 'experience' and 'nature' in broadly human terms prevented the formulation of a consistent naturalist view of nature" (ibid., p. 14). Sinclair shows how Dewey answers this narcissistic objection.

45. John Dewey, "Nature in Experience," in *1939–1941: Essays, Reviews, and Miscellany*, vol. 14 of *The Later Works of John Dewey, 1925–1953*, ed. Jo Ann Boydston (Carbondale: Southern Illinois University, 1988), pp. 142–3.

46. Ibid., p. 143.

47. Ibid.

48. In 1951, Dewey started to write a new introduction to *Experience and Nature*. He was discouraged by the obstinate refusal of his critics to understand his concept of experience and his thesis about the continuity of experience and nature: "Were I to write (or rewrite) *Experience and Nature* today I would entitle the book *Culture and Nature* and the treatment of specific subject-matters would be correspondingly modified. I would abandon the term 'experience' because of my growing realization that the historical obstacles which prevented

understanding of my use of 'experience' are, for all practical purposes, insurmountable. I would substitute the term 'culture' because with its meanings as now firmly established it can fully and freely carry my philosophy of experience" (EN 361). Dewey was greatly influenced by his Columbia colleague Franz Boas and his definition of culture: "Culture embraces all the manifestations of social habits of a community, the reactions of the individual as affected by the habits of the group in which he lives, and the products of human activities as determined by these habits" (Franz Boas, "Anthropology," in *Encyclopædia of the Social Sciences*, ed. Edwin R.A. Seligman and Alvin Johnson [New York: Macmillan, 1930], vol. 2, p. 79). For a discussion of the intertwining of culture and nature in Dewey and Boas, see Gabriel Alejandro Torres Colón and Charles A. Hobbs, "The Intertwining of Culture and Nature: Franz Boas, John Dewey, and Deweyan Strands of American Anthropology," *Journal of the History of Ideas* 76:1 (2015), pp. 139–62.

49. Godfrey-Smith and Kitcher show that what Dewey means by "instrumentalism" has little to do with contemporary uses of this expression in the philosophy of science. Both also argue that Dewey develops a distinctive type of realism (see Peter Godfrey-Smith, "Dewey on Naturalism, Realism and Science," *Philosophy of Science* 69: supp. 3 [2002], pp. S25–S35; "Dewey and the Subject Matter of Science," in *Dewey's Enduring Impact: Essays on America's Philosopher*, ed. John Shook and Paul Kurtz [Amherst, NY: Prometheus Books, 2011], pp. 73–86; and Philip Kitcher, "Deweyan Naturalism," in *Pragmatism and Naturalism: Scientific and Social Inquiry after Representationalism*, ed. Matthew Bagger [New York: Columbia University Press, 2018], pp. 66–87). For an account and defense of Dewey's realism, see Levine, "Dewey's Natural Realism," in "Meaning, Habit, and the Myth of the Given," chap. 6 of *Pragmatism, Objectivity, and Experience*, pp. 209–18.

50. For a brilliant defense of Dewey's concept of experience, see Levine, "Brandom, Pragmatism, and Experience," chap. 2 of

Pragmatism, Objectivity, and Experience, pp. 43–81. Levine argues that Rorty's and Brandom's "linguistic" critiques of Dewey fail to appreciate the significance of Dewey's (and James') theories of experience. He also forcefully argues that Brandom's account of objectivity is deficient. Levine shows the importance and relevance of Dewey's (and James') account of experience for developing an adequate pragmatic theory of objectivity.

51. See Brandom's analysis of progressive trends in classical pragmatism in PP 53–5.

52. As I have discussed above, in *Perspectives on Pragmatism* Brandom sharply criticizes Dewey for not taking "the linguistic turn" and for his failure to solve the "demarcation" problem—the demarcation between sapient and merely sentient creatures. But in his 1976 Princeton dissertation, Brandom presents a far more sympathetic account of Dewey, in which he is particularly insightful about Dewey's concept of a situation. Brandom also shows that a reconstruction of Dewey's theory of inquiry indicates how realists' and instrumentalists' claims are superseded in a pragmatic theory of social practices (see Robert Brandom, "Objects and Practices," chap. 3 of "Practice and Object" [Ph.D. diss., Princeton University, 1976], pp. 70–100).

53. For a very helpful and lucid discussion of the similarities and differences among Sellars, Brandom, and McDowell, see Chauncey Maher, *The Pittsburgh School of Philosophy: Sellars, McDowell, Brandom* (New York: Routledge, 2012).

54. Levine compares and contrasts McDowell's conception of experience with Dewey's understanding of experience in "Pragmatism, Experience, and Answerability," chap. 5 of *Pragmatism, Objectivity, and Experience*, pp. 157–91.

55. McDowell, "Naturalism in the Philosophy of Mind," in *Naturalism in Question*, p. 91.

56. John McDowell, *Mind and World: With a New Introduction by the Author* (Cambridge: Harvard University Press, 1996), p. 73;

henceforth MW, followed by page number. See also Max Weber, "Science as a Vocation," in *From Max Weber: Essays in Sociology*, trans. and ed. H.H. Gerth and C. Wright Mills (Oxford: Oxford University Press, 1946), pp. 139, 148, 155.

57. Actually, McDowell's position is more subtle. He does not claim to have a knock-down argument to show that the program of the bald naturalist *cannot* be executed. Consider how he describes his position: "I need not pretend to have an argument that the bald naturalist program—reconstructing the structure of the logical space of reasons in terms that belong in the logical space of natural-scientific understanding—*cannot* be executed. The point is just that the availability of my alternative and, I claim, more satisfying exorcism undercuts a philosophical motivation, the only one relevant to my concerns in this book, for supposing the program *must* be feasible. It is not philosophically threatening to suppose there is insight in the thought that reason is not natural, in the only sense of 'natural' countenanced by bald naturalism" (MW xxiii). Although McDowell does not make the strong claim that the bald naturalist program cannot be executed, he certainly gives good reasons for being skeptical that the program must be feasible.

58. Rouse, as we shall see, raises a number of objections to the claim that modern science is committed to the concept of nature as the "rule of law." See also Godfrey-Smith's critique of McDowell's characterization of modern science in Peter Godfrey-Smith, "Dewey, Continuity, and McDowell," in *Naturalism and Normativity*, pp. 304–21.

59. McDowell, "Naturalism in the Philosophy of Mind," p. 95.

60. McDowell never mentions Dewey when he discusses liberal naturalism.

61. Albrecht Wellmer develops a different and insightful critique of this kind of naturalism. He argues that it is "a false philosophical worldview": "But even if it is false, it could become *effective*— the enthusiasm by which it is sometimes welcomed in the mass media shows, that it is not quite ineffective. But then it could,

after all, have fatal consequences as an ideology of a psychic and social-technological practice of manipulation with deep-going and destructive consequences for democratic societies and for human freedom" (Albrecht Wellmer, "On Spirit as a Part of Nature," *Constellations* 16:2 [2009], p. 225). Dewey would certainly endorse this line of criticism about the political and moral dangers that threaten human freedom when reductive naturalism becomes an effective *ideological* force.

62. See, in particular, John Dewey, "Kant and Philosophic Method," *The Journal of Speculative Philosophy* 18:2 (1884), pp. 162–74, esp. 168.

63. See Terry Pinkard's discussion of Hegel's naturalism in his *Hegel's Naturalism: Mind, Nature, and the Final Ends of Human Life* (Oxford: Oxford University Press, 2012). For a critique of Pinkard and a defense of Hegel's naturalism that shows the affinities between Hegel's naturalism and Dewey's naturalism, see Steven Levine, "Hegel, Dewey, and Habits," *British Journal for the History of Philosophy* 23:4 (2015), pp. 632–56. See also Sebastian Rand's discussion of Hegel's *Philosophy of Nature*, and especially Hegel's understanding of second nature, in Sebastian Rand, "The Importance and Relevance of Hegel's *Philosophy of Nature*," *The Review of Metaphysics* 61:2 (2007), pp. 379–400.

64. McDowell contrasts supernatural "rampant Platonism" with a "naturalized Platonism" (MW 91–2). Naturalized Platonism is close to Aristotle's naturalism; it is the naturalism of second nature (MW 78–84).

65. McDowell, "Naturalism in the Philosophy of Mind," pp. 94–5; emphasis added.

66. Dewey writes, "Upon the whole, professed transcendentalists have been more aware than have professed empiricists of the fact that language makes the difference between brute and man. The trouble is that they have lacked naturalistic conception of its origin and status" (EN 134).

67. John Dewey, *Human Nature and Conduct: An Introduction to Social Psychology*, vol. 14 of *The Middle Works of John Dewey, 1899–1924*, ed. Jo Ann Boydston (Carbondale: Southern Illinois University Press, 1983), p. 57.

68. See John McDowell, "Wittgenstein's 'Quietism,'" *Common Knowledge* 15:3 (2009), pp. 365–72, esp. 370–1.

69. In the introduction to *Articulating the World*, Rouse states that his book "takes up the obligation for critical reflection upon human conceptual capacities at the very point where McDowell urges philosophical and scientific forbearance" (AW 13).

70. Godfrey-Smith, "Dewey, Continuity, and McDowell," p. 314.

71. Dewey's broad and deep conception of education corresponds to McDowell's *Bildung*. Consider Dewey's famous statement from *Democracy and Education*: "If we are willing to conceive education as the process of forming fundamental dispositions, intellectual and emotional, toward nature and fellow-men, philosophy may even be defined *as the general theory of education*" (John Dewey, *Democracy and Education*, vol. 9 of *The Middle Works of John Dewey, 1899–1924*, ed. Jo Ann Boydston [Carbondale: Southern Illinois University Press, 1980], p. 338). Later, I will indicate that Kitcher endorses this Deweyan claim.

72. For an excellent discussion of Dewey's concept of second nature, its Hegelian background, its relation to habit, and how it is related to ethics, art, and social criticism, see Italo Testa, "Dewey, Second Nature, Social Criticism, and the Hegelian Heritage," *European Journal of Pragmatism and American Philosophy* 9:1 (2017), http://journals.openedition.org/ejpap/990 (accessed May 3, 2019), pp. 1–23. See also Dewey's 1897 lecture on Hegel, especially his discussion of habit, in John Dewey, "Hegel's Philosophy of Spirit: 1897, University of Chicago," in *John Dewey's Philosophy of Spirit, with the 1897 Lecture on Hegel*, ed. John R. Shook and James A. Good (New York: Fordham University Press, 2010), pp. 93–176, esp. 130–1.

73. Godfrey-Smith, "Dewey, Continuity, and McDowell," p. 315.

74. McDowell explicitly rejects raising such questions as, "So what does constitute the structure of the space of reasons?" (MW 178). He writes, "If we take ourselves to be addressing that question, my invocation of second nature, sketchy and unsystematic as it is, will seem at best a promissory note toward a proper response. But that would miss my point. I think the response we should aim at being entitled to, if someone raises a question like 'What constitutes the structure of the space of reasons?,' is something like a shrug of the shoulders" (ibid.).

75. Godfrey-Smith, "Dewey, Continuity, and McDowell," p. 316. In his *Philosophy of Biology*, Godfrey-Smith writes: "Looking at biology from a philosophical point of view, one of the first things people notice is that there is apparently not much role for scientific *laws*" (Peter Godfrey-Smith, *Philosophy of Biology* [Princeton: Princeton University Press, 2014], p. 11). In a response to his critics, McDowell expresses his regret "for having aligned the distinction between first and second nature with the distinction between the realm of law and the space of reasons" (John McDowell, "Responses," in *John McDowell: Experience, Norm, and Nature*, ed. Jakob Lindgaard [Malden, MA: Blackwell, 2008], p. 220). He tells us that "there are two points to the renunciation": "First, 'the realm of law' was a bad attempt to capture the idea of a logical space that contrasts with what Sellars describes as 'the logical space of reasons.' What I wanted to bring into view was the realm of natural-scientific intelligibility, and it was wrong to suggest that all natural-scientific explanation is a matter of subsuming phenomena under law. In particular, that imposes a distorted understanding of biological intelligibility" (ibid.). But although McDowell expresses his reservations about the appeal to "the realm of law," he does *not* explicate what he means by "natural-scientific intelligibility." Later, we will see that Rouse—in a manner that has an affinity with Dewey—challenges how McDowell understands "natural-scientific intelligibility." The

second point of McDowell's renunciation is even more revealing: "Second, the idea of second nature does not line up
straightforwardly with the idea of the logical space of reasons.
Our human second nature makes us inhabitants of the logical
space of reasons. But the idea of second nature fits any pro-
pensities of animals that are not already possessed at birth,
and not acquired in merely biological maturation (like, for in-
stance, the propensity to grow facial hair on the part of male
human beings), but imparted by education, habituation, or
training. *Trained dogs have a second nature in that sense.* And the
manifestations of the second nature of a trained dog, for in-
stance obedience to commands, have an intelligibility that does
not differ interestingly from the intelligibility of manifestations of its first nature. This kind of intelligibility, even though
it attaches to phenomena of second nature, is not a matter of
placement in the logical space of reasons" (ibid.; emphasis
added). McDowell makes clear something that was not clear
in *Mind and World*: nonhuman animals have a second nature.
And it is also clear that McDowell is referring to the way in
which animals can be trained to develop habits. If McDowell
had pursued the ways in which there are continuities and differences of second nature in different types of animals, he
might have developed a Deweyan approach in which there is
continuity with difference, rather than insisting on a sharp
break between human and nonhuman animals.

76. Godfrey-Smith, "Dewey, Continuity, and McDowell," p. 316.
See also Levine's Deweyan critique of how McDowell understands the "sideways-on" view in "Meaning, Habit, and the
Myth of the Given," chap. 6 of *Pragmatism, Objectivity, and Experience*, pp. 192–234, esp. 224.

77. See John Dupré, *The Disorder of Things: Metaphysical Foundations
of the Disunity of Science* (Cambridge: Harvard University Press,
1993); "How to be Naturalistic without Being Simplistic in the
Study of Human Nature," in *Naturalism and Normativity*, pp.
289–303; and Nancy Cartwright, *How the Laws of Physics Lie*
(Oxford: Oxford University Press, 1983).

78. McDowell never provides a *detailed* analysis of what he means by "the realm of law," nor does he justify his claim that bald naturalism conceives of nature as "the realm of law."

79. In "Avoiding the Myth of the Given," McDowell states that he used to think that "to conceive experiences as actualizations of conceptual capacities, we would need to credit experiences with *propositional* content" (John McDowell, "Avoiding the Myth of the Given," in *Experience, Norm, and Nature*, p. 3). But now he rejects this assumption. He introduces the notion of "intuitional content" that is not discursive. Nevertheless, he claims that intuitional content is *conceptual*. He writes, "If intuitional content is not discursive, why go on insisting it is conceptual? Because every aspect of the content of an intuition is present in a form in which it is already suitable to be the content associated with a discursive capacity, if it is not—at least not yet—actually so associated. That is part of the force of saying, with Kant, that what gives unity to intuitions is the same function that gives unity to judgments" (McDowell, "Avoiding the Myth of the Given," p. 7).

80. In his "Afterword" to *Mind and World*, McDowell says that he has "no wish to play down the respects in which their [nonhuman animals'] lives are like ours" (MW 183). But it is also clear that McDowell shows no interest in how the scientific study of the lives of nonhuman animals might enable us to better understand how humans acquire their conceptual abilities. Despite McDowell's sharp criticisms of the dualisms that have plagued so much of modern philosophy, and despite his appeal to second nature and *Bildung*, one senses that there is a commitment to a deeper dualism that lies at the core of his thinking. McDowell insists that we humans are human *animals*. But just as our receptivity is always already conceptual, so our animality is saturated by Kantian spontaneity—"the freedom that consists in potentially reflective responsiveness to putative norms of reason" (MW 182). Consequently, there is a *radical* difference between our (human) animality and nonhuman animality. "Dumb" (nonhuman) animals lack Kantian

spontaneity. McDowell does not make any attempt to explore gradations and continuities between "dumb animals" and creatures capable of Kantian spontaneity (see, for example, MW 69–70). There is a dualism between animals that have Kantian spontaneity and those that do not. Dewey's continuity thesis challenges this radical dualism between human and non-human animals.

81. McDowell is quite explicit about this: "The way I am exploiting the Kantian idea of spontaneity commits me to a demanding interpretation for words like 'concept' and 'conceptual.' It is essential to conceptual capacities, in the demanding sense, that they can be exploited in active thinking, thinking that is open to reflection about its own rational credentials" (MW 47). In the subsequent footnote to this passage he tells us: "It is worth noting, since it helps to bring out how demanding the relevant idea of the conceptual is, that this openness to reflection implies self-consciousness on the part of the thinking subject" (MW 47n. 1). Given this "demanding" sense of the conceptual, it is absolutely clear that "brute" animals and even prelinguistic infants do *not* have concepts. McDowell never explores the possibility that there might be an important but less demanding sense of the conceptual. There is another awkward consequence of McDowell's understanding of Kantian spontaneity and his commitment to a demanding interpretation of "concept" and "conceptual." We can see this by comparing him with Sellars. When Sellars introduces the manifest image of man-in-the-world, he tells us that it is "the framework in terms of which man came to be aware of himself as man-in-the world. . . . I have given this quasi-historical dimension of our construct pride of place, because I want to highlight from the very beginning what might be called the paradox of man's encounter with himself, the paradox consisting of the fact that man could not be man until he encountered himself. It is this paradox which supports the last stand of Special Creation. Its central theme is the idea that anything which can properly be called conceptual thinking can

occur only within a framework of conceptual thinking in terms of which it can be criticized, supported, refuted, in short, evaluated. To be able to think is to be able to measure one's thoughts by standards of correctness, of relevance, of evidence. In this sense a diversified conceptual framework is a whole which, however sketchy, is prior to its parts, and cannot be constructed as a coming together of parts which are already conceptual in character. The conclusion is difficult to avoid that the transition from pre-conceptual patterns of behavior to conceptual thinking was a holistic one, a jump to a level of awareness which is irreducibly new, a jump which was the coming into being of man" (Wilfrid Sellars, "Philosophy and the Scientific Image of Man," in *Science, Perception and Reality* [Atascadero, CA: Ridgeview Publishing Company, 1963], p. 6; henceforth PSI, followed by page number). Although McDowell rejects Sellars's claim about the clash of the manifest and scientific images, he does accept the above characterization of conceptual thinking. Given McDowell's understanding of Kantian spontaneity and the demanding sense of the conceptual, he is committed to the thesis that in the course of evolution, a jump—a *radical discontinuity*—occurred with the emergence of a species that can engage in conceptual thinking. Ironically, despite his skepticism about dualisms, he affirms a *radical dualism* between human beings and the rest of nature—including all those animals that lack Kantian spontaneity. For a critique of McDowell's "intellectualism" and an alternative approach for elucidating the complexity of concepts and conceptual abilities that is more congenial to Deweyan pragmatic naturalism, see Elisabeth Camp, "Putting Thoughts to Work: Concepts, Systematicity, and Stimulus-Independence," *Philosophy and Phenomenological Research* 78:2 (2009), pp. 275–311. Dewey would certainly endorse her concluding remarks: "Conceptual thought is a wondrous thing, but as an increasing number of theorists are arguing, it does not leap full-grown, sheathed in gleaming linguistic armor, into a dull world of brute response to raw stimulus. Rather, it grows naturally out of cognitive abilities that a wide range of animals exhibit to a greater or lesser extent. It also exists alongside non-cognitive abilities that are no less sophisticated or essential for survival and flourishing. While the place of concepts in nature may be special, it is not isolated" (ibid., p. 306).

82. McDowell concedes that we share "perceptual sensitivity" with "dumb animals," but he immediately adds that there are *two species* of this perceptual sensitivity—"one permeated by spontaneity and another independent of it" (MW 69). He does not, however, explain what these two species have in common. He does not explain the *genus* that encompasses these two *species* of perceptual sensitivity. In his sixth lecture, McDowell draws upon Gadamer to indicate the difference between nonhuman animals (who lack Kantian spontaneity) and human animals: "To acquire the spontaneity of the understanding is to become able, as Gadamer puts it, 'to rise above the pressure of what impinges on us from the world'—that succession of problems and opportunities constituted as such by biological imperatives—into a 'free, distanced orientation'. And the fact that the orientation is free, that it is above the pressure of biological need, characterizes it as an orientation to the world" (Hans-Georg Gadamer, *Truth and Method*, 2nd rev. ed., trans. Joel Weinsheimer and Donald G. Marshall [New York: Crossroad, 1992], pp. 444–5; cited in MW 115–6). That is to say, nonhuman animals have an *environment*; human animals have a *world* (pp. 440–2). But even this way of distinguishing human animals from nonhuman animals reinforces a *radical dichotomy* between them. "In mere animals [nonhuman animals], sentience is in the service of a mode of life that is structured exclusively by immediate biological imperatives" (MW 115).

83. For an excellent discussion of how recent empirical and theoretical developments in evolutionary biology and philosophy support new ways of understanding language and/or conceptual capacities, see Joseph Rouse, "Conceptual Understanding as Discursive Niche Construction," pt. 1 of *Articulating the World*, pp. 39–198, esp. chap. 3, "Conceptual Understanding in

Light of Evolution," pp. 86–130. As for McDowell's claim that the attempt to give a naturalistic account of responsiveness to meaning is a "misbegotten idea" (MW 124), Jennifer Welchman develops a Deweyan rejoinder: "A pragmatic naturalistic approach to second nature diminishes its mystique, I think, but not its importance in understanding personhood, values, or practical reason. We have to give up McDowell's notion that second nature can sidestep biological determination or act outside broad constraints of natural law. But Dewey would emphasize that it allows us to 'put an end to the impossible attempt to live in two unrelated worlds' whose differences cannot be bridged" (Jennifer Welchman, "Dewey and McDowell on Naturalism, Values, and Second Nature," *Journal of Speculative Philosophy* 22:1 [2008], p. 57; Welchman is citing Dewey, *Human Nature and Conduct*, p. 11.) See also Jennifer Welchman, "Zwei Arten von Naturalismus, zweiter Natur und kommunikativen Praktiken: Eine pragmatistische Antwort auf McDowell," in *Die Gegenwart des Pragmatismus*, ed. Martin Hartmann, Jasper Liptow, and Marcus Willaschek (Berlin: Suhrkamp, 2013), pp. 223–52, for her pragmatic, naturalistic response to McDowell. Kevin Temple, in his unpublished 2017 dissertation, argues that we can reconcile two apparently conflicting ideas—that humans have the conceptual capacities to achieve rational objective knowledge of the world *and* that the same rational capacities must be in some sense continuous with other animals, most immediately with those of other great apes (see Kevin Temple, "Answering Dreyfus' Challenge: Toward a Theory of Concepts without Intellectualism" [Ph.D. diss., The New School for Social Research, 2017]). In a different way, Santiago Rey, in his unpublished 2016 dissertation, challenges McDowell's Kantian understanding of concepts (see Santiago Rey, "Worlds Made Flesh: A Stereoscopic Account of Conceptual Praxis" [Ph.D. diss., The New School for Social Research, 2016]).

84. McDowell claims that his conceptualism is based on his interpretation of Kantian spontaneity. In the past few decades,

there has been a vigorous debate about whether Kant himself was a conceptualist—and if so, what kind of conceptualist. The issue is not merely a scholarly one but raises the key question of whether it is possible to give an account of perception that does not involve concepts and yet avoids the myth of the given. For an excellent collection of recent articles dealing with conceptualist and nonconceptualist interpretations of Kant, see Dennis Schulting, ed., *Kantian Nonconceptualism* (New York: Palgrave Macmillan, 2016). Robert Hanna, in his essay "Beyond the Myth of the Myth: A Kantian Theory of Non-Conceptual Content," *International Journal of Philosophical Studies* 19:3 (2011), pp. 323–98, vigorously defends a version of nonconceptualism (nonconceptual *representational content*). He also argues that—contrary to McDowell's interpretation—Kant *endorses* nonconceptualism.

85. Although McDowell draws his ideas about spontaneity and especially his thesis that "spontaneity must structure the operations of our sensibility as such" (MW 98) from his interpretation of Kant, McDowell is not uncritical of Kant. In *Mind and World*, he writes, "Since . . . [Kant] does not contemplate a naturalism of second nature, and since bald naturalism has no appeal for him, he cannot find a place in nature for this required real connection of concepts and intuitions. And in this predicament, he can find no option but to place the connection outside nature, in a transcendental framework" (ibid.).

86. Brandom, as we have seen, criticizes Dewey for the failure to make "the linguistic turn." However, there is a downside to the way in which the linguistic turn has been understood by Sellars, Davidson, Rorty, Brandom, and McDowell. All of them accept something like Sellars's *"psychological nominalism, according to which all awareness of sorts, resemblances, facts, etc., in short, all awareness of abstract entities—indeed, all awareness even of particulars—is a linguistic affair"* (EPM 63). This leads them to claim that conceptual awareness is linguistic insofar as it is based upon or requires the mastery of discursive

language—mastering the type of linguistic abilities of creatures who can have beliefs, make judgments, and draw inferences—creatures who, in Brandom's terminology, are *sapient*. Given this tight linkage of awareness, concepts, and language, the very possibility of claiming that nonhuman animals have concepts is blocked. Sellars concedes that nonhuman animals and humans (before they acquire language) exhibit awareness-as-discriminative-behavior. But this "primitive" awareness is not conceptual. To mistake it as conceptual is to fall prey to the myth of the given. Although Rorty accepts Sellars's doctrine of psychological nominalism, he—in contrast to Brandom and McDowell—claims that this is compatible with pragmatic naturalism (see Richard Rorty, "Pre-Linguistic Awareness," in "Privileged Representations," chap. 4 of *Philosophy and the Mirror of Nature* [Princeton: Princeton University Press, 1979], pp. 182–92). For an explication and defense of Rorty's pragmatic naturalism, see Bjorn Ramberg, "Naturalizing Idealizations: Pragmatism and the Interpretivist Strategy," *Contemporary Pragmatism* 1:2 (2004), pp. 1–63. In the last few pages of his lectures, McDowell refers to Michael Dummett's claim that "the fundamental tenet of analytic philosophy is that philosophical questions about thought are to be approached through language" (Michael Dummett, "Can Analytical Philosophy be Systematic, and Ought It to Be," in *Truth and Other Enigmas* [London: Duckworth, 1978], pp. 437–58; cited in MW 124). McDowell acknowledges that, up until this point, he has "scarcely mentioned language" in his analysis of Kantian spontaneity (ibid.). Human beings are not born into the space of reasons; rather, "they are transformed into thinkers and intentional agents in the course of coming to maturity" (MW 125). He asserts that there is nothing mysterious about this transformation. "But we can take it into our stride if, in our conception of the *Bildung* that is a central element in the normal maturation of human beings, we give pride of place to the learning of *language*. In being initiated into a *language*, a human being is introduced into something that already embodies putatively rational linkages between concepts, putatively constitutive of the layout of the space of reasons, before she comes on the scene" (ibid.; emphasis added). Or, as he states later in his "Postscript to Lecture VI": "Initiation into a language is initiation into a going conception of the layout of the space of reasons" (MW 184).

87. Sinclair also criticizes McDowell (and Davidson) from a Deweyan perspective: "Davidson's and McDowell's formulations of the mind-world distinction offer strict conceptual barriers that limit or foreclose the possibility that empirical science could explain the relations between them. I have suggested that it is their philosophical conceptions of mind-nature dualism that generate this barrier or divide. But if their views make it impossible to understand how our "second nature" is related to our animal nature then we have, once again, introduced a troubling separation of humanity from nature. For Dewey this not only obscures our place within nature, but has the additional tragic consequence of preventing us from more reflective considerations about how our ability to interact with and modify nature can be better used to address the social problems we face" (Sinclair, "Anthropocentric Naturalism," p. 28).

88. Johnson, *Embodied Mind, Meaning, and Reason*, p. 39. In their Deweyan critique of Sellars and Brandom, Rebecca Kukla and Mark Lance write: "When authors such as Sellars and Brandom discuss *practices*, the lived, acting body planted in a concrete environment does not remain in view. These authors give pragmatic accounts of meaning and interpretation, but they are vastly more interested in language and theoretical reason than in the rest of human bodily activity, and they care little about how these two domains fit together" (Rebecca Kukla and Mark Lance, *'Yo! and Lo!': The Pragmatic Topography of the Space of Reasons* [Cambridge: Harvard University Press, 2009], p. 8). Despite McDowell's differences with Sellars and Brandom, and despite his claim that rationality is embodied, McDowell also fails to explore how rationality is related to "human bodily activity."

89. Peter Godfrey-Smith, "John Dewey's *Experience and Nature*," *Topoi* 33:1 (2014), p. 290. Godfrey-Smith's "belated" review of Dewey's *Experience and Nature* is one of the best and clearest discussions of this book. He focuses on Dewey's contributions to metaphysical and epistemological issues and shows how these are related to contemporary debates and discussions.

90. See ibid., p. 285. Godfrey-Smith stresses how his interpretation of Dewey—especially how his reading of *Experience and Nature* (and other writings from the 1920s and 1930s)—differs from Rorty's. Rorty is not only dismissive of Dewey's attempt to elaborate a descriptive metaphysics; he argues that Dewey's appeal to experience is so unwieldly that pragmatists should drop talk about experience and limit themselves to language (ibid., p. 289). Brandom, Rorty's student, follows Rorty's advice. Brandom tells us that in his *magnum opus, Making It Explicit*, he *mentions* experience but never *uses* it as a philosophical concept (PP 197). The concept of experience plays no role in his version of a linguistic rationalistic pragmatism. This dismissal of experience has led to an extensive debate between those who claim that the appeal to experience was not only central to all the classical American pragmatists but is essential for developing a viable pragmatic naturalism and those who argue that pragmatism today must take the linguistic turn. Most recently, there has been a strong reaction against advocates of linguistic pragmatism. Levine argues that both Rorty and Brandom fail to appreciate the nuances of Dewey's (and James') concepts of experience. Furthermore, he argues that Brandom's attempt to develop a pragmatic concept of objectivity is a failure: we cannot develop an adequate pragmatic naturalistic theory of objectivity without an appeal to experience (see Levine, "Rorty and the Rejection of Objectivity," chap. 1 of *Pragmatism, Objectivity, and Experience*, pp. 21–42; and chap. 2 in the same volume, "Brandom, Pragmatism, and Experience," pp. 43–81). On the issue of the debate about language and experience for pragmatism, see my "Experience after the Linguistic Turn," chap. 6 of *The Pragmatic Turn* (Malden, MA: Polity, 2010), pp. 125–52.

91. See Godfrey-Smith, "Dewey on Naturalism, Realism, and Science," pp. 25–35; "Dewey and the Subject Matter of Science," pp. 73–86; and "John Dewey's *Experience and Nature*," pp. 285–91. During the first part of the twentieth century, Dewey was criticized by both American "realists" and American "idealists." For a historical discussion of these criticisms and Dewey's responses to them, see David L. Hildebrand, *Beyond Realism and Antirealism: John Dewey and the Neopragmatists* (Nashville: Vanderbilt University Press, 2003). Hildebrand also argues that the neo-pragmatic debate about realism and antirealism by Putnam and Rorty distorts Dewey's position, which is "beyond" realism and antirealism (pp. 177–94).

92. See Peter Godfrey-Smith, *Other Minds: The Octopus, the Sea, and the Deep Origins of Consciousness* (New York: Farrar, Straus and Giroux, 2016), esp. pp. 164–70.

93. See especially, Godfrey-Smith, "From White Noise to Consciousness," chap. 4 of *Other Minds*, pp. 77–105.

94. Dewey tends to restrict the term "mind" to humans but would certainly be open to the way in which Godfrey-Smith speaks of the minds of nonhuman animals.

95. For a comprehensive and lucid account of Dewey's conception of philosophy, see Philip Kitcher, "Dewey's Conception of Philosophy," in *The Oxford Handbook of Dewey*, ed. Steven Fesmire (Oxford: Oxford University Press, 2017), pp. 3–21.

96. See Philip Kitcher, "The Importance of Dewey for Philosophy (and for Much Else Besides)," in *Preludes to Pragmatism: Toward a Reconstruction of Philosophy* (Oxford: Oxford University Press, 2012), p. 2.

97. Philip Kitcher, "From Naturalism to Pragmatic Naturalism," introduction to *Preludes to Pragmatism*, pp. xiv–v.

98. Ibid., p. xviii.

99. Ibid., pp. xv–vi.

100. For Kitcher's naturalistic and humanistic account of religion, see Philip Kitcher, *Life after Faith: The Case for Secular Humanism* (New Haven: Yale University Press, 2014).

101. Dewey, *Democracy and Education*, p. 338; cited in Kitcher, "The Importance of Dewey for Philosophy," p. 1.

102. Kitcher, "Deweyan Naturalism," p. 68.

103. Ibid.

104. Dewey would be sympathetic with the distinction that Price draws between two kinds of naturalism, but I think he might object to the terminology of "subject naturalism" and "object naturalism" because of the traditional epistemological overtones of the expressions "subject" and "object."

105. Huw Price, "Naturalism without Representationalism," in *Expressivism, Pragmatism and Representationalism* (Cambridge: Cambridge University Press, 2013), pp. 4–5; henceforth NWR, followed by page number.

106. Price identifies "subject naturalism" with the naturalism of Hume and "arguably Nietzsche" (NWR 5), but it is certainly also the naturalism of Dewey.

107. Beginning with Peirce, pragmatists have always been critical of epistemological and semantic forms of representationalism. This theme is continued by those contemporary pragmatists who have taken the linguistic turn and direct their criticism to versions of semantic representationalism. There have been "in house" debates about whether anything can be salvaged from representational theories. Rorty holds the most extreme view. He wants to dump all versions of representationalism (see, for example, Richard Rorty, "Anti-Representationalism, Ethnocentrism, and Liberalism," introduction to *Objectivity, Relativism, and Truth*, vol. 1 of *Philosophical Papers* [Cambridge: Cambridge University Press, 1991], pp. 1–18). Price and Brandom (although they disagree with each other) nevertheless want to preserve something from the linguistic versions of representationalism. In an email to Price, Rorty writes: "As you

might have expected, my doubts are all about whether you are radical enough. I am not sure that it is worthwhile retaining lower-case representationalism by means of your notion of 'internal representations,' just as I am unsure whether it was a good strategy for Brandom to try to revivify representational- ist notions within the bosom of his inferentialism" (Richard Rorty, email message to Huw Price, May 19, 2006; cited in Price, "Prospects for Global Expressivism," in *Expressivism, Pragmatism and Representationalism*, p. 193). Rorty also explicitly expresses his sympathy with Price's distinction between "sub- ject naturalism" and" object naturalism" and his claim that "subject naturalism" has priority. Rorty points out how Ram- berg's pragmatic naturalism follows the same approach (see Richard Rorty, "Naturalism and Quietism," in *Naturalism and Normativity*, p. 59). Both Price's subject naturalism and Ram- berg's pragmatic naturalism support Dewey's thesis about continuity. Ramberg (in a statement that echoes Dewey) says: "Naturalization . . . is a goal of philosophy; it is the elimination of metaphysical gaps between the characteristic features by which we deal with agents and thinkers, on the one hand, and the characteristic features by reference to which we empirically generalize over the causal relations between objects and events, on the other" (Ramberg, "Naturalizing Idealizations," p. 43; cited in Rorty, "Naturalism and Quietism," p. 59).

108. See Richard J. Bernstein, "Dewey's Naturalism," *The Review of Metaphysics* 13:2 (1959), pp. 340–53.

109. Sellars makes it clear that he is using "image" in a very broad sense—as "things imagined," or more accurately, as "*conceived*" (PSI 5). I suspect that if Sellars were writing today, he might speak of "humans-in-the-world" rather than "man-in-the- world."

110. Sellars is perfectly aware that these two images are artificial ideal constructs that are employed for heuristic purposes. He compares them to Weberian ideal types (PSI 5). For example,

correlational and postulational techniques have been inter-twined throughout history, but Sellars stipulates that "postulational theory construction" belongs exclusively to the scientific image. "Our contrast then, is between two ideal con-structs: (a) the correlational and categorial refinement of the 'original image,' which refinement I am calling the manifest image; (b) the image derived from the fruits of postulational theory construction which I am calling the scientific image" (PSI 19). In this essay (and other places), Sellars makes it clear that he is defending scientific realism against the varieties of scientific instrumentalism. This means that those entities and/or processes that eventually turn out to be the primary objects of the scientific image are the entities and/or pro-cesses that constitute *reality*.

111. There is something extremely odd about the way in which Sellars introduces the clash of the two images. Up until this point in his essay, Sellars has characterized the manifest image and the scientific image as "images," "conceptions," or "frameworks." Now he poses the question: "How, then, are we to evaluate the *conflicting claims* of the manifest image and the scientific image thus provisionally interpreted to constitute the *true* and, in principle, *complete* account of man-in-the-world?" (PSI 25; first emphasis added). This is a paradoxical question since Sellars now ascribes *agency* to each of the im-ages; they make claims, indeed, conflicting claims. But presumably it is only persons that have the *intentionality* to make claims. Persons are the primary objects of the manifest image. It would seem that if it is legitimate to speak about the two images making "conflicting claims," then both images are pre-supposing the category of persons—those objects or entities that have the capacity to make claims. If we add something that Sellars says later in this essay, that it is impossible—*logically impossible*—to reconstruct the category of persons in the sci-entific image (see PSI 38–9), then it seems impossible to avoid the conclusion that the scientific image that makes the *claim* to be the *true* and *complete* account of man-in-the-world *presupposes*

the type of entity that can make claims—i.e., persons. This is not merely a methodological presupposition but rather a *substantive* one. Only persons (not images) have the intentionality required to make claims about what constitutes "the *true* and in principle, *complete* account of man-in-the-world" (ibid.).

112. Wilfrid Sellars, "The Language of Theories," in *Science, Perception and Reality*, p. 121.

113. Earlier, following Rorty, I distinguished left Sellarsians from right Sellarsians. Left Sellarsians rarely even discuss "Philosophy and the Scientific Image." They treat it as one of Sellars's more unfortunate papers. They are drawn primarily to Sellars's *Empiricism and the Philosophy of Mind*—the attack on the myth of the given, the exploration of conceptual thinking, language, meaning, thinking, and perception from the manifest point of view. For left Sellarsians, this is Sellars's canonical text. Rorty, in his pungent and polemical style, expresses his disdain for the Sellarsian attempt to develop a synoptic vision that joins the scientific and manifest images: "Despite my veneration for Wilfrid Sellars, who originated this talk of manifest and scientific images, I would like to jettison these visual metaphors. We should not be held captive by the world-picture picture. We do not need a synoptic view of something called 'the world.' At most, we need a synoptic narrative of how we came to talk as we do. We should stop trying for a unified picture, and for a master vocabulary. We should confine ourselves to making sure that we are not burdened with obsolete ways of speaking, and then insuring that those vocabularies that are still useful stay out of each other's way" (Rorty, "Naturalism and Quietism," p. 58).

114. Willem deVries, James O'Shea, and Sachs develop this more centrist interpretation (see Willem A. deVries, *Wilfrid Sellars* [Montreal: Queens's University Press, 2005]; James O'Shea, *Wilfrid Sellars: Naturalism with a Normative Turn* [Malden, MA: Polity, 2007]; and Sachs, *Intentionality and the Myths of the Given*).

One of the great obstacles to providing a coherent interpretation of Sellars's synoptic vision is making sense of precisely what Sellars means by "picturing" (see Wilfrid Sellars, "Being and Being Known," in *In the Space of Reasons: Selected Essays of Wilfrid Sellars*, ed. Kevin Scharp and Robert B. Brandom [Cambridge: Harvard University Press, 2007], pp. 218–9). Sachs develops one of the clearest interpretations of the meaning and importance of picturing in Sellars. He argues that Sellars makes a sharp distinction between signifying and picturing, and that picturing enables us to grasp what Sellars appropriates from Dewey's naturalism: "Put most generally, picturing is the ability to reliably track and respond to causal regularities in the environment. As such it is distinguished from what Sellars calls 'signifying,' or the ability to engage in intentional discourse and distinctively structured thought. Sellars's relation to the history of pragmatism can be most clearly seen if we see him as aligned with Dewey with regards to picturing and with Lewis with regards to signifying" (Carl B. Sachs, "'We Pragmatists Mourn Sellars as a Lost Leader': Sellars's Pragmatist Distinction between Signifying and Picturing," in *Sellars and the History of Modern Philosophy*, ed. Luca Corti and Antonio M. Nunziante [New York: Routledge, 2018], p. 162).

115. Rouse's book has an illuminating discussion of the Dreyfus-McDowell debate. He shows how, to a great extent, the two are speaking past each other because they have radically different ideas about conceptual understanding. Rouse characterizes Dreyfus' approach as "operative-process" and McDowell's as "normative-status": "I do not follow Dreyfus in thinking of practical-perceptual coping as a distinct, preconceptual 'level' of intentional directedness. Yet I also do not simply endorse McDowell's therapeutic acceptance of conceptual normativity as pervasive even in perception. Despite insisting upon a normative account of the conceptual domain, I will draw upon considerations from Dreyfus' work to place conceptual normativity within a scientific understanding of nature" (AW 50).

116. Rouse points out that that these thinkers "endorse a minimalist naturalism, arguing that nothing in their views is *inconsistent* with what we learn from the natural sciences. Conceptual normativity nevertheless remains autonomous in their view, without need or expectation of further scientific explication" (AW 14).

117. For the details of Rouse's understanding of scientific practice and how it relates to conceptual normativity, see his "Conceptual Articulation in Scientific Practice," pt. 2 of *Articulating the World*, pp. 199–342. It is important to underscore how Rouse's practice-oriented understanding of science departs from many standard conceptions of science accepted by philosophers. For example, De Caro and Macarthur contrast scientific naturalism with the "newly emerging hopes for another, philosophically more liberal, naturalism" (De Caro and Macarthur, "The Nature of Naturalism," p. 1). They claim that there are two important and characteristic themes of scientific naturalism: "(1) *An Ontological Theme*: a commitment to an exclusively scientific conception of nature; (2) *A Methodological Theme*: a reconception of the traditional relation between philosophy and science according to which philosophical inquiry is conceived as continuous with science" (p. 3). But they do not clearly explain what they mean by "science" and by "an exclusively scientific conception of nature." They seem to rely on a commonly accepted understanding of science. The reason why this is important is that if we accept their contrast between scientific naturalism and a more philosophically liberal conception of naturalism, we are tempted to conclude that a liberal naturalism is not scientific. But Rouse argues that with a more open-ended, practice-oriented understanding of science, we can show that those things that left Sellarsians exclude from science—our conceptual abilities (and all that they entail)—are amenable to scientific understanding. Dewey would certainly agree with Rouse. Too frequently, when philosophers speak of "scientific naturalism," they have in mind only those sciences (for example, physics) that do not treat the

distinctive features of human beings in their organic-environment interactions.

118. See also Rouse, "Scientific Significance," chap. 10 of *Articulating the World*, pp. 317–41.

119. Dewey would completely agree with the following statement that appears in "Naturalism and the Contingency of the Space of Reasons," the epilogue to Rouse's book: "Sciences are historically specific practices that emerged within human history, with significance and justificatory standards that continue to change. This recognition ought to broaden the scope of philosophical reflection upon the sciences" (AW 383). Rouse's concluding sentences sound like Dewey's call for a reconstruction of philosophy: "Who we are and shall be; what our world is like and how it might further reveal itself; and what possibilities it might thereby open to us and our descendants or close off: those are at issue and at stake in the ongoing development of our social-discursive way of life, including out scientific practices. Nothing could matter more, or be less arbitrary from a naturalistic standpoint, from *within* the world that we live in and seek to understand" (AW 386).

120. See the Appendix, where I show that Wilfrid Sellars was thoroughly familiar with the evolutionary naturalism and the critical realism of his father, Roy Wood Sellars.

121. Although Putnam affirms his Kantian affinities, he consistently challenged the nature/norm dichotomy and the fact/value dichotomy (see Hilary Putnam, *The Collapse of the Fact/Value Dichotomy and Other Essays including the Rosenthal Lectures* [Cambridge: Harvard University Press, 2002]).

122. Kitcher articulates Dewey's view of the relation of scientific "posits" and the objects that we encounter in everyday life: "The scientist hypothesizes an abstract atom or an abstract electron, conceived as having all and only the properties in a specified set, and, on this basis, is able to organize particular phenomena (e.g., chemical reactions or radioactive decay).

Conceived as a model, the posit is a useful tool. When the success of the positing becomes sufficiently pronounced, scientists often regard themselves as having discovered a new constituent of reality, and, in his realist moments, Dewey is happy to follow them in this. What disturbs him is the supposition that these constituents have *exactly the properties ascribed to them in the scientist's model and no more*. For that conjures up a world of allegedly 'fundamental' constituents, one that displaces the qualities rightly ascribed to everyday things. *EN* [*Experience and Nature*] and *QC* [*The Quest for Certainty*] are intent on resisting the remaking of reality in the image of theoretical models, but that does not in any way preclude Dewey from supposing that macroscopic things are made up of microscopic constituents, constituents that *include* among their properties those ascribed in the abstract description. Those constituents also have the properties of giving rise, under the appropriate conditions, to the manifest qualities ('blue,' 'sweet,' and so forth). Dewey . . . can, quite consistently, assert that the macroscopic table is 'the only table'— denying the existence of something made up of the abstract posits of the model—while affirming that that sole real table is made up of tiny constituents, whose interactions generate its familiar properties and which have among their properties the qualities the model ascribes to them" (Kitcher, "Deweyan Naturalism," p. 77).

123. Roy Wood Sellars, *Evolutionary Naturalism* (Chicago: Open Court, 1922), p. 21; cited in Fabio Gironi, "A Kantian Disagreement between Father and Son: Roy Wood Sellars and Wilfrid Sellars on the Categories," *Journal of the History of Philosophy* 55:3 (2017), p. 524.

124. See "Humanist Manifesto I," American Humanist Association, https://americanhumanist.org/what-is-humanism/manifesto1/ (accessed December 1, 2019).

125. See Gironi, "A Kantian Disagreement between Father and Son," pp. 513–36.

126. Ibid., p. 513.

127. Wilfrid Sellars, "Physical Realism," *Philosophy and Phenomenolog-ical Research* 15:1 (1954), p. 13; cited in Gironi, "A Kantian Disagreement between Father and Son," p. 515.

128. From 1958 until 1963, when Sellars was a professor of philosophy at Yale University, I was a junior member of the Philosophy department. I had the good fortune to attend many of his graduate seminars. In 1966, I published a two-part article in *The Review of Metaphysics*, "Sellars' Vision of Man-in-the-Universe," based primarily on the papers included in *Science, Perception and Reality* and some of his earlier articles. This was one of the earliest attempts to outline Sellars's comprehensive, synoptic, and stereoscopic vision that he was in the process of developing. Although written more than fifty years ago, I think that my exposition and the perplexities that I expressed are still relevant (see Richard J. Bernstein, "Sellars' Vision of Man-in-the-Universe I," *The Review of Metaphysics* 20:1 [1966], pp. 113–43; and "Sellars' Vision of Man-in-the-Universe II," *The Review of Metaphysics* 20:2 [1966], pp. 290–316). See also Price's illuminating discussion of Sellars's struggle in articulating what precisely he means by "description" in Price, "Prospects for Global Expressivism," pp. 160–70. In the famous Chisholm-Sellars correspondence, Chisholm expresses his skepticism about Sellars's use of the "technical philosophical term 'descriptive.'" He cites Sellars's claim: "'My solution is that " '. . .' means . . ." is the core of the unique mode of discourse which is as distinct from the *description* and *explanation* of empirical fact as is the language of *prescription* and *justification*'" (Wilfrid Sellars and Roderick M. Chisholm, "Chisholm-Sellars Correspondence on Intentionality," in *Intentionality and the Mental*, appendix to *Concepts, Theories, and the Mind-Body Problem*, vol. 2 of *Minnesota Studies in the Philosophy of Science*, ed. Herbert Feigl, Michael Scriven, and Grover Maxwell [Minneapolis: University of Minnesota Press, 1958], p. 529). Chisholm then comments: "I am inclined to feel that the technical philosophical term 'descriptive' is one which is very much over used, and I am not sure I can attach much meaning

to it. Indeed I would be inclined to say that if the locution 'Such and such a sentence is *not* descriptive' means anything at all, it means that the sentence in question (like 'Do not cross the street' and 'Would that the roses were blooming') is neither true nor false" (ibid.). In his response to Chisholm, Sellars writes: "I . . . agree that the term 'descriptive' is of little help. Once the 'journeyman' task (to use Ayer's expression) is well under way, it may be possible to give a precise meaning to this technical term. (Presumably this technical use would show some measure of continuity with our ordinary use of 'describe')" (ibid., p. 532).

129. Willem A. deVries, "Images, Descriptions, and Pictures: Personhood and the Clash," in *Sellars and His Legacy*, ed. James O'Shea (Oxford: Oxford University Press, 2016), p. 52.

130. Ibid.

131. Ibid., p. 53.

132. Wilfrid Sellars, "Phenomenalism," in *In the Space of Reasons: Selected Essays of Wilfrid Sellars*, p. 341.

133. Ibid.

134. See Kant, *Critique of Pure Reason*, A367–80. Kant shows here how "the transcendental idealist is an empirical realist" (A371).

135. DeVries, "Images, Descriptions, and Pictures," p. 58.

136. Willem A. deVries, "Language, Norms and Linguistic Norms," in *Wilfrid Sellars, Idealism, and Realism: Understanding Psychological Nominalism*, ed. Patrick J. Reider (London: Bloomsbury, 2017), p. 83.

137. Ibid., p. 98.

138. Ibid.; emphasis added.

139. DeVries, *Wilfrid Sellars*, p. 277; emphasis added.

140. Ibid.

REFERENCES

Baldwin, James Mark, *Handbook of Psychology: Feeling and Will* (New York: Henry Holt and Company, 1894).

Bernstein, Richard J., "Dewey's Naturalism," *The Review of Metaphysics* 13:2 (1959), pp. 340–53.

————, *John Dewey* (Atascadero, CA: Ridgeview Publishing Company, 1966).

————, "Sellars' Vision of Man-in-the-Universe I," *The Review of Metaphysics* 20:1 (1966), pp. 113–43.

————, "Sellars' Vision of Man-in-the-Universe II," *The Review of Metaphysics* 20:2 (1966), pp. 290–316.

————, *The Pragmatic Turn* (Malden, MA: Polity, 2010).

Boas, Franz, "Anthropology," in *Encyclopædia of the Social Sciences*, ed. Edwin R.A. Seligman and Alvin Johnson (New York: Macmillan, 1930), vol. 2, pp. 73–110.

Brandom, Robert, "Practice and Object" (Ph.D. diss., Princeton University, 1976).

————, *Perspectives on Pragmatism: Classic, Recent, and Contemporary* (Cambridge: Harvard University Press, 2011).

Camp, Elisabeth, "Putting Thoughts to Work: Concepts, Systematicity, and Stimulus-Independence," *Philosophy and Phenomenological Research* 78:2 (2009), pp. 275–311.

Cartwright, Nancy, *How the Laws of Physics Lie* (Oxford: Oxford University Press, 1983).

Cohen, Morris R., "Some Difficulties in Dewey's Anthropocentric Naturalism," *Philosophical Review* 49:2 (1940), pp. 196–228.

De Caro, Mario and Macarthur, David, "The Nature of Naturalism," in *Naturalism in Question*, ed. Mario De Caro and David Macarthur (Cambridge: Harvard University Press, 2004), pp. 1–17.

—————, "Science, Naturalism, and the Problem of Normativity," in *Naturalism and Normativity*, ed. Mario De Caro and David Macarthur (New York: Columbia University Press, 2010), pp. 1–19.

deVries, Willem A., *Wilfrid Sellars* (Montreal: Queens's University Press, 2005).

—————, "Images, Descriptions, and Pictures: Personhood and the Clash," in *Sellars and His Legacy*, ed. James O'Shea (Oxford: Oxford University Press, 2016), pp. 47–59.

—————, "Language, Norms and Linguistic Norms," in *Wilfrid Sellars, Idealism, and Realism: Understanding Psychological Nominalism*, ed. Patrick J. Reider (London: Bloomsbury, 2017), pp. 83–100.

Dewey, John, "Kant and Philosophic Method," *The Journal of Speculative Philosophy* 18:2 (1884), pp. 162–74.

—————, "Experience, Knowledge, and Value: A Rejoinder," in *The Philosophy of John Dewey*, ed. Paul Arthur Schilpp, vol. 1 of *The Library of Living Philosophers*, ed. Paul Arthur Schilpp et al. (New York: Tudor Publishing Company, 1958), pp. 515–608.

—————, "The Present Position of Logical Theory," in *1889–1892: Essays and Outlines of a Critical Theory of Ethics*, vol. 3 of *The Early Works of John Dewey, 1882–1898*, ed. Jo Ann Boydston (Carbondale: Southern Illinois University Press, 1969), pp. 125–41.

—————, "The Reflex Arc Concept in Psychology," in *1895–1898: Early Essays*, vol. 5 of *The Early Works of John Dewey, 1882–1898*, ed. Jo Ann Boydston (Carbondale: Southern Illinois University Press, 1972), pp. 96–109.

—————, *Democracy and Education*, vol. 9 of *The Middle Works of John Dewey, 1899–1924*, ed. Jo Ann Boydston (Carbondale: Southern Illinois University Press, 1980).

————, "The Need for a Recovery of Philosophy," in *1916–1917: Journal Articles, Essays, and Miscellany Published in the 1916–1917 Period*, vol. 10 of *The Middle Works of John Dewey, 1899–1924*, ed. Jo Ann Boydston (Carbondale: Southern Illinois University Press, 1980), pp. 3–49.

————, *Experience and Nature*, vol. 1 of *The Later Works of John Dewey, 1925–1953*, ed. Jo Ann Boydston (Carbondale: Southern Illinois University Press, 1981).

————, "From Absolutism to Experimentalism," in *The Philosophy of John Dewey: Two Volumes in One*, ed. John J. McDermott (Chicago: University of Chicago Press, 1981), pp. 1–13.

————, "The Influence of Darwinism on Philosophy," in *The Philosophy of John Dewey: Two Volumes in One*, ed. John J. McDermott (Chicago: University of Chicago Press, 1981), pp. 31–41.

————, *Human Nature and Conduct: An Introduction to Social Psychology*, vol. 14 of *The Middle Works of John Dewey, 1899–1924*, ed. Jo Ann Boydston (Carbondale: Southern Illinois University Press, 1983).

————, "The Inclusive Philosophic Idea," in *1927–1928: Essays, Reviews, Miscellany, and "Impressions of Soviet Russia,"* vol. 3 of *The Later Works of John Dewey, 1925–1953*, ed. Jo Ann Boydston (Carbondale: Southern Illinois University Press, 1984), pp. 41–54.

————, *Logic: The Theory of Inquiry*, vol. 12 of *The Later Works of John Dewey, 1925–1953*, ed. Jo Ann Boydston (Carbondale: Southern Illinois University Press, 1986).

————, "Nature in Experience," in *1939–1941: Essays, Reviews, and Miscellany*, vol. 14 of *The Later Works of John Dewey, 1925–1953*, ed. Jo Ann Boydston (Carbondale: Southern Illinois University, 1988), pp. 141–54.

————, "Hegel's Philosophy of Spirit: 1897, University of Chicago," in *John Dewey's Philosophy of Spirit, with the 1897 Lecture on Hegel*, ed. John R. Shook and James A. Good (New York: Fordham University Press, 2010), pp. 93–176.

————, "Lecture III: The Social Value of Education as Reconstructive Control over One's Experience," in pt. 1 of *Education, Logic, Ethics, and Political Philosophy*, vol. 2 of *The Class Lectures of John Dewey, Electronic Edition*, 2nd release, ed. Donald F. Koch and The Center for Dewey Studies (Carbondale: Southern Illinois University, 2015), http://www.nlx.com/collections/441 (accessed October 14, 2019).

Dummett, Michael, "Can Analytical Philosophy be Systematic, and Ought It to Be," in *Truth and Other Enigmas* (London: Duckworth, 1978), pp. 437–58.

Dupré, John, *The Disorder of Things: Metaphysical Foundations of the Disunity of Science* (Cambridge: Harvard University Press, 1993).

————, "How to be Naturalistic without Being Simplistic in the Study of Human Nature," in *Naturalism and Normativity*, ed. Mario De Caro and David Macarthur (New York: Columbia University Press, 2010), pp. 289–303.

Gadamer, Hans-Georg, *Truth and Method*, 2nd rev. ed., trans. Joel Weinsheimer and Donald G. Marshall (New York: Crossroad, 1992).

Gironi, Fabio, "A Kantian Disagreement between Father and Son: Roy Wood Sellars and Wilfrid Sellars on the Categories," *Journal of the History of Philosophy* 55:3 (2017), pp. 513–36.

Godfrey-Smith, Peter, "Organism, Environment, and Dialectics," in *Thinking about Evolution: Historical, Philosophical, and Political Perspectives*, ed. Rama S. Singh, Costas B. Krimbas, Diane B. Paul, and John Beatty (Cambridge: Cambridge University Press, 2001), vol. 2, pp. 253–66.

————, "Dewey on Naturalism, Realism and Science," *Philosophy of Science* 69: supp. 3 (2002), pp. S25–S35.

————, "Dewey, Continuity, and McDowell," in *Naturalism and Normativity*, ed. Mario De Caro and David Macarthur (New York: Columbia University Press, 2010), pp. 304–21.

————, "Dewey and the Subject Matter of Science," in *Dewey's Enduring Impact: Essays on America's Philosopher*, ed. John Shook and Paul Kurtz (Amherst, NY: Prometheus Books, 2011), pp. 73–86.

————, "John Dewey's *Experience and Nature*," *Topoi* 33:1 (2014), pp. 285–91.

————, *Philosophy of Biology* (Princeton: Princeton University Press, 2014).

————, *Other Minds: The Octopus, the Sea, and the Deep Origins of Consciousness* (New York: Farrar, Straus and Giroux, 2016).

Hanna, Robert, "Beyond the Myth of the Myth: A Kantian Theory of Non-Conceptual Content," *International Journal of Philosophical Studies* 19:3 (2011), pp. 323–98.

Hildebrand, David L., *Beyond Realism and Antirealism: John Dewey and the Neopragmatists* (Nashville: Vanderbilt University Press, 2003).

"Humanist Manifesto I," American Humanist Association, https://americanhumanist.org/what-is-humanism/manifesto1/ (accessed December 1, 2019).

Johnson, Mark, *Embodied Mind, Meaning, and Reason: How Our Bodies Give Rise to Understanding* (Chicago: University of Chicago Press, 2017).

Kant, Immanuel, *Kritik der reiner Vernunft (1787)*, ed. Benno Erdmann, vol. 3 of *Werke*, ed. Wilhelm Dilthey, vols. 1–9 of *Gesammelte Schriften* (Berlin: De Gruyter, 1911).

————, *Critique of Pure Reason*, trans. and ed. Paul Guyer and Allen W. Wood (Cambridge: Cambridge University Press, 1999).

Kitcher, Philip, *Preludes to Pragmatism: Toward a Reconstruction of Philosophy* (Oxford: Oxford University Press, 2012).

————, *Life after Faith: The Case for Secular Humanism* (New Haven: Yale University Press, 2014).

————, "Dewey's Conception of Philosophy," in *The Oxford Handbook of Dewey*, ed. Steven Fesmire (Oxford: Oxford University Press, 2017), pp. 3–21.

————, "Deweyan Naturalism," in *Pragmatism and Naturalism: Scientific and Social Inquiry after Representationalism*, ed. Matthew Bagger (New York: Columbia University Press, 2018), pp. 66–87.

Levine, Steven, "Hegel, Dewey, and Habits," *British Journal for the History of Philosophy* 23:4 (2015), pp. 632–56.

————, *Pragmatism, Objectivity, and Experience* (Cambridge: Cambridge University Press, 2019).

Maher, Chauncey, *The Pittsburgh School of Philosophy: Sellars, McDowell, Brandom* (New York: Routledge, 2012).

McDowell, John, *Mind and World: With a New Introduction by the Author* (Cambridge: Harvard University Press, 1996).

————, *Mind, Value, and Reality* (Cambridge: Harvard University Press, 1998).

————, "Naturalism in the Philosophy of Mind," in *Naturalism in Question*, ed. Mario De Caro and David Macarthur (Cambridge: Harvard University Press, 2004), pp. 91–105.

————, *Experience, Norm, and Nature*, ed. Jakob Lindgaard (Malden, MA: Blackwell, 2008).

————, "Wittgenstein's 'Quietism,'" *Common Knowledge* 15:3 (2009), pp. 365–72.

O'Shea, James, *Wilfrid Sellars: Naturalism with a Normative Turn* (Malden, MA: Polity, 2007).

Pearce, Trevor, *Pragmatism's Evolution: Organism and Environment in American Philosophy* (Chicago: University of Chicago Press, 2020).

Peirce, Charles Sanders, *Principles of Philosophy*, ed. Charles Hartshorne and Paul Weiss, vol. 1 of *Collected Papers of Charles Sanders Peirce* (Cambridge: Harvard University Press, 1965).

Pinkard, Terry, *Hegel's Naturalism: Mind, Nature, and the Final Ends of Human Life* (Oxford: Oxford University Press, 2012).

Price, Huw, *Expressivism, Pragmatism and Representationalism* (Cambridge: Cambridge University Press, 2013).

Putnam, Hilary, *The Collapse of the Fact/Value Dichotomy and Other Essays including the Rosenthal Lectures* (Cambridge: Harvard University Press, 2002).

————, *Naturalism, Realism, and Normativity*, ed. Mario De Caro (Cambridge: Harvard University Press, 2016).

Quine, W.V.O., *Ontological Relativity and Other Essays* (New York: Columbia University Press, 1969).

————, *Theories and Things* (Cambridge: Harvard University Press, 1981).

Ramberg, Bjorn, "Naturalizing Idealizations: Pragmatism and the Interpretivist Strategy," *Contemporary Pragmatism* 1:2 (2004), pp. 1–63.

Rand, Sebastian, "The Importance and Relevance of Hegel's *Philosophy of Nature*," *The Review of Metaphysics* 61:2 (2007), pp. 379–400.

Rey, Santiago, "Worlds Made Flesh: A Stereoscopic Account of Conceptual Praxis" (Ph.D. diss., The New School for Social Research, 2016).

Rorty, Richard, *Philosophy and the Mirror of Nature* (Princeton: Princeton University Press, 1979).

————, "Comments on Sleeper and Edel," *Transactions of the Charles S. Peirce Society* 21:1 (1985), pp. 39–48.

————, *Objectivity, Relativism, and Truth*, vol. 1 of *Philosophical Papers* (Cambridge: Cambridge University Press, 1991).

————, "Naturalism and Quietism," in *Naturalism and Normativity*, ed. Mario De Caro and David Macarthur (New York: Columbia University Press, 2010), pp. 55–68.

————, *Mind, Language, and Metaphilosophy: Early Philosophical Papers*, ed. Stephen Leach and James Tartaglia (Cambridge: Cambridge University Press, 2014).

Rouse, Joseph, *Articulating the World: Conceptual Understanding and the Scientific Image* (Chicago: University of Chicago Press, 2015).

Ryder, John, (ed.), *American Philosophic Naturalism in the Twentieth Century* (Amherst, NY: Prometheus Books, 1994).

Sachs, Carl B., *Intentionality and the Myths of the Given: Between Pragmatism and Phenomenology* (London: Routledge, 2016).

————, "'We Pragmatists Mourn Sellars as a Lost Leader': Sellars's Pragmatist Distinction between Signifying and Picturing," in *Sellars and the History of Modern Philosophy*, ed. Luca Corti and Antonio M. Nunziante (New York: Routledge, 2018), pp. 157–77.

Särkelä, Arvi, *Immanente Kritik und soziales Leben: Selbsttransformative Praxis nach Hegel und Dewey* (Frankfurt: Klostermann, 2018).

Schulting, Dennis, (ed.), *Kantian Nonconceptualism* (New York: Palgrave Macmillan, 2016).

Sellars, Roy Wood, *Evolutionary Naturalism* (Chicago: Open Court, 1922).

Sellars, Wilfrid, "Physical Realism," *Philosophy and Phenomenological Research* 15:1 (1954), pp. 13–32.

————, *Science, Perception and Reality* (Atascadero, CA: Ridgeview Publishing Company, 1963).

————, *Empiricism and the Philosophy of Mind* (Cambridge: Harvard University Press, 1997).

————, *In the Space of Reasons: Selected Essays of Wilfrid Sellars*, ed. Kevin Scharp and Robert B. Brandom (Cambridge: Harvard University Press, 2007).

Sellars, Wilfrid and Chisholm, Roderick M., "Chisholm-Sellars Correspondence on Intentionality," in *Intentionality and the Mental*, appendix to *Concepts, Theories, and the Mind-Body Problem*, vol. 2 of *Minnesota Studies in the Philosophy of Science*, ed. Herbert Feigl, Michael Scriven, and Grover Maxwell (Minneapolis: University of Minnesota Press, 1958), pp. 507–39.

Sinclair, Robert, "Anthropocentric Naturalism," in *Pragmatism, Science, and Naturalism*, ed. Jonathan Knowles and Henrik Rydenfelt (Frankfurt: Peter Lang, 2011), pp. 13–30.

Stroud, Barry, "The Charm of Naturalism," in *Naturalism in Question*, ed. Mario De Caro and David Macarthur (Cambridge: Harvard University Press, 2004), pp. 21–35.

Temple, Kevin, "Answering Dreyfus' Challenge: Toward a Theory of Concepts without Intellectualism" (Ph.D. diss., The New School for Social Research, 2017).

Testa, Italo, "Dewey, Second Nature, Social Criticism, and the Hegelian Heritage," *European Journal of Pragmatism and American Philosophy* 9:1 (2017), pp. 1–23, http://journals.openedition.org/ejpap/990 (accessed May 3, 2019).

Torres Colón, Gabriel Alejandro and Hobbs, Charles A., "The Intertwining of Culture and Nature: Franz Boas, John Dewey, and Deweyan Strands of American Anthropology," *Journal of the History of Ideas* 76:1 (2015), pp. 139–62.

Weber, Max, *From Max Weber: Essays in Sociology*, trans. and ed. H.H. Gerth and C. Wright Mills (Oxford: Oxford University Press, 1946).

Welchman, Jennifer, "Dewey and McDowell on Naturalism, Values, and Second Nature," *Journal of Speculative Philosophy* 22:1 (2008), pp. 50–8.

————, "Zwei Arten von Naturalismus, zweiter Natur und kommunikativen Praktiken: Eine pragmatistische Antwort auf McDowell," in *Die Gegenwart des Pragmatismus*, ed. Martin Hartmann, Jasper Liptow, and Marcus Willaschek (Berlin: Suhrkamp, 2013), pp. 223–52.

Wellmer, Albrecht, "On Spirit as a Part of Nature," *Constellations* 16:2 (2009), pp. 213–26.

Wenley, Robert Mark, *The Life and Work of George Sylvester Morris: A Chapter in the History of American Thought in the Nineteenth Century* (New York: Macmillan, 1917).

www.ingramcontent.com/pod-product-compliance
Lightning Source LLC
Chambersburg PA
CBHW070639030426
42337CB00020B/4086